THE CRAFT OF THE
CLASSROOM

*Other Books for Teachers by
the same author*

TOWARDS THE NEW FIFTH
Longman

THE PRACTICE OF ENGLISH TEACHING
(with Graham Owens) Blackie

HEAD OF DEPARTMENT
Heinemann

PASTORAL CARE
Heinemann

CURRICULUM AND TIMETABLE OF THE SECONDARY SCHOOL
Heinemann

and for Pupils

PETER GRIMES
Heinemann

ENGLISH FOR THE INDIVIDUAL
(with Denys Thomson) Heinemann

THE QUESTION OF ADVERTISING
Chatto and Windus Educational

STUDENT DRAMA SERIES
Blackie

IMPRINT BOOKS
Longman

The Craft of the Classroom

*A survival guide to classroom management
in the Secondary School*

MICHAEL MARLAND
Headmaster
Woodberry Down School
London

HEINEMANN EDUCATIONAL BOOKS
LONDON

Heinemann Educational Books Ltd

LONDON EDINBURGH MELBOURNE AUCKLAND TORONTO
HONG KONG SINGAPORE KUALA LUMPUR
IBADAN NAIROBI JOHANNESBURG
LUSAKA NEW DELHI

ISBN 0 435 80577 0

Published by
Heinemann Educational Books Ltd
48 Charles Street, London W1X 8AH
Photoset and printed by
Interprint (Malta) Ltd

Contents

Acknowledgements

Although I am responsible for any failures in conception, argument, example or expression, I should like to thank those of my colleagues past and present from whom I have learnt, and the following, who made helpful criticisms of the book in draft: Shirley Hase, Ian Leslie, Sylvia Richardson, and George Walker.

M. M.

To the pupils I have taught,
still teach, and will teach,
whom I have learnt to like more
as I have learnt to manage
them better

1 Starting Points

The core of Secondary-school education is what happens day in and day out in the ordinary classrooms. Whatever a school may devise or an LEA supply, whatever extra-curricular activity may flourish, or whatever counsellors there may be, it is in the classroom interchange of teacher and taught that a school's success or failure is gained. We may take on board new curricular schemes, we may embrace more subtle educational philosophies, we may deepen our understanding of the sociology of our environment, establish a rich network of links with our community, and devise stunningly ingenious timetables – but everything centres round the classroom.

The more you look at schooling in practice, the more you study research and observation, and the more you consider the real problems of helping the young learn, the more you are forced to the simple conclusion that individual teachers are the most important factor. It is not the school organization, the syllabus, or the teaching method, except in so far as they help or hinder the individual teacher.

Yet the success of the individual teacher depends on more than impressive personality and learning. Whatever his subject and whatever teaching method he is adopting, the teacher is essentially a group worker. There is an art in managing the group in a Secondary-school classroom that is vital for the pupils. Every teacher must be proficient in this art. The encouraging thing is that it can be learnt, practised and improved. It is not merely 'natural', and when it has been acquired you and your pupils will enjoy your time together in school more.

Sadly, it has to be said that this is a truth that has been to a considerable extent overlooked in the last decade. The controversy over Secondary reorganization and the enthusiasm for curriculum development have obscured the fact that both depend on successful classroom conditions. As education has increasingly become a newsworthy subject, so the peripheral aspects of education, which are inherently more attractive to journalists, have become dominant. Articles have been written about educational television, relationships with parents, integrated studies, teaching machines, and a hundred and one other interesting and important topics, but very few people have looked at the daily interchange in the classroom. This is the real life of education.

Here things have not been going too well. The pressure for change has kept schools alive with ideas, but has undoubtedly produced tension and even confusion. Staff turnover has increased for social and financial reasons, so that learning on the job is harder. Reorganization has thrown immensely heavy administrative and planning burdens on schools. Social and geographical mobility have increased and led to more frequent movement of pupils. Inner-city social conditions have deteriorated rapidly. A general 'decline in deference' has made it harder to look after young people. It is not that they have become 'tougher' or more 'violent', but they have certainly become more choosey, less easy to organize, less easy to impress, and less easy to lead (and yet still wanting leadership!) at a time when we have decided to keep the whole age range in school until they are sixteen-plus. New styles of bringing up children from babyhood, new economic standards, the availability of impressive television programmes and lavish magazines, the range of goods in the shops, have all contributed to create a style in young people that is less amenable to many aspects, some of them essential, of schools.[1] The considerable expansion of the teaching force has put burdens on the teacher educators, as well as bringing a wider range of people into teaching, many of them expecting something different, easier, more varied than the job actually is.

In some ways there has been far too much talk of the 'dedication' of teachers and there is often a self-conscious 'commitment'. Concern for children and commitment to helping them are necessary but not sufficient conditions for success. Even love has to have method. Some teachers whose commitment has not been self-evident or overpowering have achieved great success through patient and methodical professionalism. Others with all the fervour have had little success.

There is no doubt that conditions in the classrooms are frequently not good, and that, whilst in many ways education has advanced substantially in the last decade, the craft of teaching has not been cherished in initial training, in-service courses,

[1] I have discussed 'The Clients and their Times' in some detail in chapter 3 of my *Pastoral Care*, Heinemann Educational Books, 1974.

professional literature, or educational journalism. Yet, as the classroom remains the centre of education and is likely to do so, the central art of a teacher is to manage that classroom. This book is an attempt to bring the classroom back to the centre of the educational focus and to sketch some elements of the craft of its management.

In this book, I have in mind helping both student teachers in training and those in their early years of teaching. Probably the current changes in the scheme of teacher education, with the extended training 'on the job' in the Induction Year, will tend to merge the two conditions of student and fully-fledged teacher. The new process should be more practical. Certainly, the gradual creation of 'Professional Tutors' will give young teachers the precise help which they greatly need. There will still be a need, however, for a clear account of classroom management. I hope that every student or teacher going into his or her first teaching practice or first job will find this short account helpful.

The Individual and the Craft

Like every other teacher, you and I are individuals with personalities of our own and teaching approaches which are special to us. Certainly no one can take over another teacher's ways lock, stock, and barrel, apply them, and hope for success. No doubt you will do some extraordinary things that I should not dare to do, and no doubt you will get away with some of them. *But* there are many techniques of class management for the Secondary school that can be distilled from the work of hundreds of teachers and have almost universal validity. These are not techniques that will cramp your style, but ones that will allow it to flower. The paradox is that good classroom management makes *personal* teaching possible, for it frees the individual from constant conflict, and only then can the teacher be truly personal. Good organization in the classroom avoids confrontation, and allows the teacher to establish the warm relationships with most of his pupils that he wants.

The central point is obvious: everything depends on good order. Without it every lesson will be a battle. You will be exhausted; your pupils will behave badly, and later criticize *you*. If you establish good order, you can be more subtle, more friendly, and more yourself. You regularly find in schools pupils who defy and taunt any teachers who are apparently unable to control them, and then complain bitterly to parents and senior teachers that they don't like those teachers' classes: 'He doesn't keep us in order!' There is no doubt in my mind that a very large proportion of adolescent pupils will try to drive a teacher to distraction; if they succeed they will despise him or her and hate the conditions they have helped to create. Contrary to superficial impressions, most, very nearly all, pupils like good order, and are happier if the classroom is 'in control'. The very word 'control' is unfashionable and has pejorative associations. Yet a teacher must face up to the fact that 'controlling' is part of his task, and if he fails in that he will fail in much else. There is no way in which you can avoid influencing children, and control is certainly not abused just because it is practised. If a teacher's psychological make-up is such that he finds the notion repugnant, he should re-consider his profession. In this context it is worth noting that something has gone wrong with the popularly presumed definitions of words like 'liberal'. Every teacher wants to be considered 'liberal', and many are confused by the apparent synonymity in some people's minds with 'permissive', 'easy-going', etc. Caricatures of past Headmasters, who, it was alleged, were happy only if every classroom was absolutely silent, have encouraged many teachers to feel that they are committing a sin against progressive education if they ever insist that the classroom is silent. They learn to live with noise, and forget that the teacher who can manage to put up with interruptive noise is often imposing unpleasant and unaccept-able conditions upon pupils who cannot. One of the most important freedoms which a school can offer to pupils is free-dom from the noise of others, the interruptions of others, and their own restlessness. Of course, good order is certainly not an end in itself, but do not in any way underestimate its value as an aid to your more important aims.

Despite the question often asked about a young teacher, 'How's his discipline?', there is no single, readily identifi-able characteristic 'discipline'. The pupils know which teachers 'keep us in order', and those teachers are the ones they respect. The pupils can not usually identify what it is about a parti-cular teacher that leads to this quality they admire of keeping order. Pushed, pupils will offer such helpful clues as 'Well, he means what he says', 'He knows what he's doing', 'She don't let us muck about', 'We have to get on with things with her'. The insistent questioner will probably put the major part of the elusive quality down to 'personality', and no book is going to get far trying to teach that. But a careful questioner will also detect at least three other strands amongst the pupils' descriptions of the teachers whom they judge to be a success.

One will be a sense of caring, of never giving up. The successful teacher knows that some of his hopes are rarely attainable, but he is not daunted. The pupils sense that this teacher cares and that he will keep on trying, and that he respects them. This sense of caring is also conveyed clearly to the pupils in the other sense of whether the teacher 'cares for' them, the second strand. Many teachers with high ideals actually fail to feel sufficient care for their charges. Love alone cannot guarantee success, but it is necessary – a rather hard, remote, balanced, ungushing kind of love.

The third strand the questioner will pick up from the pupils' remarks is that simple one of good basic teaching: 'She makes things clear'. Some people try hard to get close to the pupils, sympathize with their problems, and chat with them, but they fail in their fundamental task of making complicated things simple, of explaining in ways that can be understood, of *teaching*. Again, this book cannot hope to go very far towards that aim, although some sections (e.g. pages 70–78) will, I hope, be helpful.

The fourth, and final, strand, however, is the one with which this book is most fully concerned: a good teacher is a good classroom manager. Whatever mode of teaching he is employing, and whatever subject matter or skill is being explored, a teacher has the major task of managing the classroom. This involves control of the group, the manipulation of time, the organization of learning materials, and it also involves the teacher's own voice and manner. The book argues that this craft is a necessary one for the teacher, and one about which much can be taught and learnt. The craft of the classroom is something at which you can work and at which you can get better. In doing so you will not only increase your control of the classroom, but, perhaps paradoxically, you will also find yourself giving less attention to class management, getting closer to the pupils, teaching more helpfully, and, above all, enjoying the pupils more. Good relationships are to some extent an ingredient of successful classroom management, but to a considerable degree they are also the *result*. There is more crossness, shouting and criticism in a badly run classroom than a good one. The well-organized teacher is in a better position to be pleasant to his pupils. A mastery of group management techniques frees a teacher from concerns about group control.

Some of the procedures I have outlined in this book are

easier to describe than to do. Practice will make them possible but you will find the task easier for pre-planning. One of the paradoxes of classroom management is that some initial fuss often reduces subsequent fuss; that some apparently complicated initial procedures actually simplify procedures in the long run; that formal routines free the sessions for close relationships. To be organized and firm is to have cleared the decks for variety of activity and friendliness, but to be slightly confused and wavering is to produce a muddle that will lead only to frayed tempers, cross words, less pupil enjoyment, and less learning. All this is especially true with less well-motivated and with 'difficult' children. For them your technique must be impeccable. I have seen teachers trying to muddle through for years: it doesn't work. If, on the other hand, you analyse an aspect of classroom management to establish what makes it difficult, you will usually see where the difficulty lies; and be able to go a long way towards avoiding it next time round. For instance, contrary to many of our easily adopted attitudes, it isn't the presence of two or three troublesome pupils that makes it difficult to get a lesson started. It is an inherently difficult task whatever the composition of the pupil group, and some teachers would run into difficulties with a hand-picked class of obliging pupils. With any pupils, your class management skill must be as polished as possible. Have no doubt, though, that this is a skill, can be learnt, and does matter.

There are five kinds of preparation you need to undertake before receiving the first pupils:

a. Find out about the school, its structure and procedures, and your department and syllabus. I discuss this in chapter 8.
b. Find out about the pupils you will be teaching. I discuss this in chapter 2.
c. Prepare your classroom. I discuss this in the first part of chapter 3.
d. Prepare your registers. I discuss this in chapter 4.
e. Prepare your textbooks and equipment. I discuss this in chapter 5.

There is, then, a craft of classroom management, which is independent not only of subject, but also of mode of teaching. Whatever you are teaching, *and however you plan to teach*, you must run a good classroom.

2 The Relationships of the Classroom

Of all the sections of this book, clearly the one in which I attempt to discuss how to create 'good relationships' with pupils is the most difficult. Here is the nub of the teacher's task, yet it is the most difficult to define, the most personal to achieve, and the most intangible to judge. Advice can easily be mis-applied, and remarks parodied. Yet I must attempt the task, both because it is so important and because I believe that the creation of good classroom relationships is actually more amenable to technical advice than it may seem to be. It is not luck but method which brings success. Good relationships are in fact *created*.

In the first place, don't presume that it is as easy as all that; don't presume that you are the first pleasant person who has come the way of these hard-done-by pupils; and, above all, don't presume that your *will* to create good relationships will prove sufficient. You will need to work at it patiently and skil-fully; you will need to have a long-term perspective; and you will need to have created an orderly and systematic classroom procedure which allows the good relationship. The old saying 'Never smile before Easter' was an exaggeration that neverthe-less had a germ of good psychological sense in it. There is a very great danger in adopting too rapidly a permissive attitude to the class in the search for immediate popularity. I don't wish to undervalue the aim, but the result is usually to lose esteem in the medium- and long-term, and to encourage bad behaviour. It suggests that there is no scale of values, and thus no especial way in which approval can be won.

One of the apparent paradoxes of teaching is that the 'strict teacher' often proves to have a more friendly classroom than the easy-going teacher. Indeed, the strict teacher usually shouts less (pupils hate being shouted at) and has fewer rows (also hated) than all but the most easy-going teacher. The strict teacher creates the peace which is necessary for any positive relationship.

Secondly, focus quite clearly on the obvious but easily overlooked fact that it is as a *teacher* that you are hoping to create a relationship. The teaching is not only the object of the exercise, it is also the special gift that you have for the pupil and which most of the other people to whom the pupil relates have not got. This is both a proud claim and a modest one. It is arrogant to forget that, although on occasions you will do some mothering, most of your pupils have splendid mothers; although on occasions you will be matey, most of your pupils have close friends with whom they spend hours; although on occasions you will be avuncular, most of your pupils have adequate uncle figures. Do not let your knowledge of the very sad cases of some children from broken, confused, or uncaring homes tempt you into forgetting that the majority of pupils have warm and supportive homes. Do not allow your wish to be a friend to come between you as teacher and pupil: if you cannot succeed as a teacher your friendship is unlikely to be of special value to the young person. A teacher opens up unknown or only half-suspected areas of skill or knowledge; he makes things clear; he makes things as simple as possible. He enables pupils to do more things and to do them better, to understand more things and to understand them better. Only if you are felt to be successful in these teacherly ways will the pupils warm to you. It is therefore doubly misjudged to allow the wish for 'a good relationship' to hinder effective teaching.

In this respect it is also important to avoid a well-meant but essentially patronizing social 'determinism' that allows teachers to collude with pupils from less well-off backgrounds to avoid real learning as 'irrelevant' or beyond them. In the last decade teachers have become far more socially aware. There are few of us who have not read the important analyses of the educational sociologists. This is on the whole a distinct gain. However, for some young teachers it can get between them and their task. It is easy to misuse sociological information, especially analyses of the characteristics of social class. We now know a great deal of the educational handicaps of children of unskilled and semi-skilled workers, not to mention immigrants, one-parent families, and other deprived groups. This knowledge can be misused to create an oversimplified kind of 'determinism', which is allowed to trap pupils in their current plight: 'You can't expect high literacy standards. Look at their homes', or 'There's nothing relevant in the curriculum for them, so naturally they aren't motivated to do homework'.

Such attitudes are helpful only if they are used to sharpen our techniques and create sympathy. They are dangerous if they lead us to treat pupils as if school had nothing but sympathy to offer. For these pupils as much as any others, the teacher must teach and must maintain with cheerful determination the aim of making learning possible.

Thirdly, you will want to consider continuously the motivation of the classroom. We have rightly elevated motivation to a high priority in our planning. It is important, however, that in searching for improved motivation we do not overlook the very basic point that in fact almost the best motivation is simply achievement. On the whole, we want to do the things we can do, and don't want to do the things we can't do. In classroom terms this means that it is not practical to put too much emphasis on motivation, nor to wait until pupils 'are motivated' to do something. Vigorous teaching of the skills will often lead on to motivation. 'Being able' to do is very close to 'wanting' to do. Not being able to do is distressingly off-putting.

I think that the child-centred 'interest' model has done a great deal of good to education, but I must point out that it is not only inadequate in itself, but also can be positively harmful if misunderstood. We tend to presume that learning is its own reward, and that the best form of motivation is to re-shape the curriculum so that the learning can be more relevant. As adults we have four main reward systems: money, usefulness, status, the gratitude or approval of those we live with. The teenager, poised functionless in the world, has few possible rewards in school. Money is only a useful motivation for some aspects of some subjects (and there is a limit to the possible extension of this reward system); status is in a way available; it is, however, the gratitude or approval of those we live with that is the most potent: the second greatest motivation (that is, after achievement) is the pupil's relationship with his teachers. School is a part of life (not mere preparation), and works only if it offers human warmth and satisfaction. The teacher's task is to recognize this and build it into his systems. By using this, he can both make the learning more effective *and* create a satisfying social life.

Fourthly, as a teacher with responsibility for a *group* of pupils, you are inevitably a leader. You have to be able to dominate the group. Obviously this is an ability that has to be used tactfully and sensitively – but it must be possible. It is pointless to be afraid of 'dominating' the pupils, whether for the sake of creating good relationships or from a wish to allow individuality to flourish.

There is amongst many young teachers a diffidence that makes them pull back from imposing their will: the result, too often, is that a clique of pupils in the class imposes its will instead. This is resented by the other pupils, and the resentment sours those pupils' relationship with the teacher. Diffidence is a virtue in many circumstances, but it is dangerous in the classroom: it often allows those who are not diffident – and there are likely to be a few in every group – to dominate. This leads to tension, conflict, rows, and in the end to a less pleasant and tighter domination by the teacher if he can achieve it. If not, the situation is left unresolved in a plethora of bad temper.

There is also a very understandable fear which many teachers have of losing the affection or good relationship of pupils. This fear makes the teachers, like timid lovers, apprehensive lest the first dark look is evidence of favours withdrawn for ever. The contemporary stress on creating good relationships with those being taught can be self-defeating if it leads the teacher to go for quick results, and encourages him to reduce his demands in the hope of easier returns. There is nothing so pathetic as the sight of the desperately anxious teacher casting away more and more of his standards as frantic sops to rapid popularity and sacrificing the elements essential to a good long-term relationship to the empty hopes of immediate success. Teaching is a reasonably long-term activity, and the relationships that succeed will be built up by a long-term policy. The pupil is always suggesting that he will withdraw his affection from the teacher, like the child from his parent, unless a demand is dropped. If your demand is legitimate and for the pupil's good, don't be tempted to abandon it. The relationships at which you should be aiming are those achieved by, say, the end of the year, not the end of the first week.

Getting to Know Your Pupils

The first task is to learn their names. It really helps if you know each of your pupils by his or her correct name as early as possible – and that means getting the abbreviations and diminutives right too. A few initial mistakes don't actually matter. They are inevitable, and accepted by the pupils as evidence that you are trying. You should laugh at your mistakes, and come back to another attempt fairly soon. For years I used to blandly write my memory off as 'never good with pupils' names', as if it was a regrettable but inevitable inherent failing. The result was that I had unnecessary difficulties with classes for far too long. I now realize that there are positive steps you can take to help yourself. In particular, study the list of pupils in advance, and when you are copying it into your mark book, or on to seating plans, etc., try to memorize the Christian name-surname combinations. It helps to know as many of these as possible even before you've met the pupils. When you study the records and files, use this also as a conscious name-learning session. In the classroom (and your seating plan helps here) do not lean back on the fact that you haven't yet learnt the names by pointing at pupils whom you want to speak. Use names from the very first by glancing down at your seating plan. Some teachers ask pupils, especially younger classes, to make name cards for their desks. These can also help. Give back exercise books yourself as part of your memorization.

You will rarely or never get to know pupils as people via the whole group or with the whole group present. Obviously, your observation of each of them in the group context will contribute massively to your knowledge of each individual pupil. Equally obviously, you will learn a great deal from your reading of the writing or exercises which are done for you. Clearly, you will need to supplement this direct observation by studying the background of each pupil. This can be time-consuming if done thoroughly, but as each year you stay at the school you carry forward your knowledge of many of the pupils, the problem becomes less difficult. The two obvious ways of filling in on the background of your pupils are by consulting the files or record cards (either those held by your department or those held by the pastoral organization) and by discussing the list of pupils with the pastoral figure (Tutor or Form Master) of each class. The snag about this method is that if you aren't careful you will get only confirmation of your own observation of the more obvious classroom traits. However, if you specifically ask for background details, and not classroom behaviour, you will glean much helpful information. If you have six classes, as you may, my advice is that you should methodically enquire about each group in turn at the rate of about two a week, and should be satisfied with a fairly short session to get the basic material you need. Make a jotting of each point, however briefly, for you will never remember all that you pick up. Some schools, by the way, have specially convened meetings of all the teachers concerned with a particular group of pupils. These are sometimes chaired by the Tutor, sometimes by a Head of Year, Head of House, or more senior member of staff. Obviously such meetings are of immense value in sharing knowledge of each pupil. Take these opportunities, and as often as possible talk to your colleagues about the pupils.

Despite the importance of methodically using these ways of getting to know your pupils, there is obviously nothing as valuable as personal knowledge. This comes from your using every possible opportunity to talk individually, or, at the most, with two pupils at a time. There will be some chances within the lesson as you circulate or call pupils to sit by you. But these moments must be built upon by creating as many additional out-of-school moments as possible. Start this as soon as you can by asking one or two members of the group to stay behind afterwards, perhaps to help you with some legitimate task, perhaps just to talk over their work. Don't make a dead set at the very start at the handful of obviously difficult pupils, but on the other hand do try to get to those for a chat fairly early on. And then, don't overdo it: you are not going to find out all their secrets and establish a warm, lasting relationship in five minutes of arranging a wall display or chatting over a piece of homework. You have succeeded well enough if you get to know your chosen pupils just a little more than you did. Let them know that on your own and without a class to control you are mildly human and well meaning. Then you have begun to break down that frightening 'class' into individuals. By patiently working at each and every opportunity, you will gradually build up a close knowledge of each pupil, and will find that when you are working with the whole class, in addition to the class management lines, you have also, as it were, a series of private lines, a rich network of personal relationships of different degrees of strength. Everything you do to further extend and deepen this network will prove to be of great help and satisfaction to you.

One unexpected source of knowledge will come your way, if you make the effort, through your responsibilities under whatever 'duty' rota system your school runs. It is too easy, but quite wrong, to think of a teacher's supervisory 'duties' as mere chores that in some utopia will be handed over to other figures. I should say that playground, corridor, or lunch-hall duties are essentially *teaching* activities. They are opportunities for relating to pupils in a variety of contexts. A duty is a flop if you just stand and look on coolly. You can find out about individual pupils by stopping to exchange a word, or by having an extended conversation. You will find out how to speak to pupils in joke or in anger, and how to influence them with good grace. Although supervisory duties can be difficult, you will learn a great deal without the constraints of the classroom, without problems of class management, and without the demands of their learning.

Supervisory duties are often a strain to young teachers, who find it difficult to establish their role and are frankly nervous about precisely how observant they should be, how strict they should be, and what manner they should adopt. In the first place, it is important to remember that the bunch of unknown boys whom you see lurking in that funny corner behind the gyms might well be your responsibility in a classroom soon, either in a regular class of yours or in a lesson you are having to take for an absent teacher. When you do so meet them, they will remember their playground encounter. If you avoid them, obviously unsure of your ground, they will take their future cue from your present behaviour. You must weigh in to any trouble or incipient trouble that you see, however slight or however serious. Try to check in advance precisely what is allowed and what is not (e.g. Is the grass protected? Can ball games be played anywhere?). Move definitely but calmly towards any group of pupils, especially if they are in odd corners or recesses. Go in smiling, if possible making a joke or a cheerful conversational remark. Unless there is clearly harm being done, don't necessarily investigate. Keep the conversation going and disperse the group good-humouredly. If you do see any misbehaviour (e.g. fighting or damage to the building), act firmly. If you are very new and don't know the pupils, send another pupil for the senior teacher likely to be available. If you feel you can cope, tell the pupils suspected of the bad behaviour to come with you to the senior teacher.

There is one whole range of activities which deserves special mention as a way of getting to know pupils – the many things that live under the vague title 'extra-curricular activities'. It is probably wise in your first year not to devote too much precious energy to extra-curricular activities, and certainly not to over-burden yourself with the taxing worry of actually organizing or leading such an activity. Nevertheless, I would really stress that it is in the shared enthusiasms of camping, producing plays, tidying books, playing chess, looking after animals, kicking a ball around, or going to the theatre that teacher and taught can come closest together. This will be a valuable investment for you in two ways. On the one hand, you will have a sprinkling of allies in various parts of the school with whom you have bonds forged in their special cherished circumstances. And on the other hand, you will have learned a great deal about young people, their reactions and their moods. You will have learnt how to speak to pupils in a variety of contexts, when to quip and when to be serious, when to turn a blind eye and when to be eagle-eyed, when to muck in and when to rise above. Above all, you will have learnt how to lay down limits and say 'No' when necessary, in ways which are acceptable. You will, it is true, have learnt all this with a rather special selection of pupils, but what you will have learnt can be applied to your relations with all of them. I should go as far as to say that you will never succeed in the classroom if you have not gained that special dimension from some extra-curricular activities.

Consistency

It is harder in fact than in theory to establish a reasonably consistent regime, but it is essential to do so if you are to create good relationships. Pupils like to know where they are with their teachers, and not be pulled up one day for what they were allowed to get away with the day before. Agreement between teachers is difficult to achieve and less essential. Obviously a wildly different set of expectations between teachers is not desirable, but just as pupils accept differences between codes in laboratories and libraries, so they expect and can accept a certain degree of difference between teachers. A school should work towards reducing these differences by discussion and debate, but obviously they will never be removed completely. This the pupils will accept. But they do *not* find differences within a single teacher's behaviour acceptable. 'Moody' is a serious criticism, and justifiably so. To be allowed to talk after a 'Silence' one day, but to be reprimanded for the same talking in the same situation the following day causes confusion and resentment. Try hard to set an unvarying standard. *Always* get cross with late-comers; *always* make a fuss about home-work not brought; never accept talking during a declared 'silent' session; and so on. If your rules are reasonable, stick to them day in and day out.

When all is said and done, however, you will have to vary your approach to suit the individuals you teach. You must be consistent from occasion to occasion, but flexible from individual to individual. One of the specialisms of a school is that of knowing pupils. You will subtly vary your approach to each as you get to know him or her. With one you will need to remain always light-hearted, with another quiet and personal. One may require only a look, another a sharp remark. You will learn that some pupils react badly to public rebuke, some can't stand praise in public, others won't answer questions aloud however hard you press, whilst some will try to answer a question before you have even asked it. Many pupils behave acceptably but cannot resist subtly baiting to provoke. The teacher who knows those pupils intimately knows how to side-step the provocation, retain his dignity and authority, and maintain a warm relationship. All of this requires a great flexibility of approach to individuals.

Be determined. A teacher must never give up. If your pupils know that you know clearly and without doubt who has not done something, their confidence in your knowledge is the first, and remarkably successful, 'disciplinary' influence you have. The second is their certainty that, like a terrier with his teeth in a slipper, you will not give up. Most pupils are canny enough to know that with many teachers a 'forgotten' piece of homework not brought one day will mean the end of the matter. If it is clear that the teacher will remember and ask for it the following day – and keep on until it has been obtained – the number of intitial lapses of memory drops impressively. In general, never let anything go by you and there will be less to chase. The more fuss you make, the less you will have to fuss about.

Praise and Criticism

Undoubtedly, we all are happier and do better when we are praised rather than criticized. Much of what I have said in previous sections has been designed to put pupils in situations in which they can legitimately be praised and to keep them out of situations in which they are likely to behave badly and thus bring criticism on themselves from even the mildest or most forbearing of teachers. If this has been achieved, make sure that the ratio of praise to censure remains squarely in favour of praise. Both individuals and the class as a whole need to be commended for their achievements.

It is easy to overlook the occasions for praise, and to react more rapidly to the need to censure. Remember to praise the ordinary. Personal praise is certainly possible – a boy dressed particularly smartly, his new hair-cut, a girl's new hair-style, a new school bag, a well-labelled exercise book. Each lesson, you should try to find some word of praise for a handful of fairly ordinary but commendable things: a well-answered question, the good use of a word, a helpful act.

There are three audience contexts for praise, and they should all be used for really good effect. Firstly, there is the public praise in front of the other pupils. This is usually much appreciated, but should not be overdone or loosely fulsome. Secondly, there is the quiet private word with the individual pupil. This is too often forgotten. Sometimes it should be used to reinforce the first, perhaps on the way out at the end of the lesson. Thirdly, there is the communication of praise by note or entry in the school *Diary* for the parent or Tutor (Form Teacher) to see. Again, don't forget this very helpful act.

Be careful how you praise the regular public troublemaker. If, as is so often the case, he is seeking group status by his ostentatious misbehaviour, he will resent the public praise as an attack on his reputation, and as likely as not he will find some technique of expression or gesture that not only nullifies the praise but, worse than that, actually associates your praise with his scorn – thus devaluing it for others. He can publicly 'do dirt' on your commendation, and this is potentially dangerous for the future. This does not, however, normally mean that he does not want the praise, merely that he doesn't want it openly. For such a pupil the private word of praise is essential, and frequently effective.

Generally speaking, when censure is required give it clearly but briefly, do not dwell on it and, above all, avoid the tirade of abuse directed at an individual. Such a tirade creates a deep resentment in the individual so that, far from being persuaded to mend his ways, he will harden against you and feel justified in his action. Added to that, other individuals will sympathize with the victim in his plight, and you will have lost the good-will of a whole section of the class. Whenever you respond publicly to a pupil, you must also have in mind the ripple effect on the other pupils.

Don't focus over-sharply on the regular troublemakers. An American theorist[1] dubs one technique 'extinction'. He means

[1] Clarizio, Harvey F., *Towards Positive Classroom Discipline*, John Wiley & Sons, 1971.

by this the ignoring of the troublesome behaviour to avoid rewarding it by taking notice. This is a line which should be used only with care – but it reminds one that it is possible to actually reinforce bad behaviour by giving it excessive attention.

Whenever possible, influence the misbehaving pupil, or the pupil about to misbehave, silently and without the rest of the class knowing. Perhaps a small gesture will catch his eye; more likely a stare will be sensed and he will look up. Then a mere continuation of the stare may be sufficient, but it can be strengthened by a frown, or even a smile. This last may sound surprising, but a smile indicates you know the pupil was up to something he shouldn't have been, that you are not furious – yet, and that if he stops all will be well. A mouthed but soundless word or two can also be added occasionally. Such tactics avoid advertising the unsuitable behaviour to other pupils, and avoid the attendant risk of encouraging others to join in. They also avoid the teacher adding his voice to the disturbance. This even creates a conspiratorial feeling between the teacher and the would-be wrong-doer that leaves a pleasurable rather than a thwarted feeling in the pupil. One warning, though: if you use the stare as a device, don't be out-stared back – you must win. These points apply especially in group work or individual work in mixed-ability classes.

Many disturbances that are minor but nevertheless require more than a look or silent gesture are quelled easily by the teacher who shows he or she is anxious to get on with the job in hand and is not willing to wast time investigating. A Science teacher moving towards a group whose experiment is being held back by giggles over something one of the boys has produced from his pocket, would actually be best advised to say as he arrived at the group: 'Come on; we just haven't got time for that', and immediately ask an interesting question about the experiment. In general, it is more effective to use what has been called 'task-focused' criticisms rather than 'approval-focused', especially as far as the effect on other pupils is concerned:

'Ray, if you talk you won't be able to hear these new words so well'

is normally better than:

'Ray, I'm surprised at you letting me down again'.

Criticisms and prohibitions must be clear. It is amazingly easy to convey a general sense of disapproval without making it clear exactly what is being objected to. American research has demonstrated that that clarity of reprimands is of more importance that their intensity. Thus:

'Don't touch that display board' is more likely to be effective than:

'Behave yourself.'

and:

'Leave Gary's desk alone.'

is more likely to be effective than:

'Stop fooling around.'

Your bluff will usually be called, so don't throw out empty threats of punishments you can't in fact carry out. Some teachers use excessive physical threats: 'If you don't sit down, I'll hit you', when it is neither permitted nor desirable to do so. These both undermine your authority and create an unpleasant atmosphere. (I am excepting the *clearly* jocular threats which really are meant to be, and are, taken as jokes to relieve class tension: 'Do that again, and I'll hang you by your feet out of the window!') Similarly, if you know you have to hurry away after school one day, don't threaten to keep a pupil in unless you are willing to forgo that appointment. Always keep your word to your pupils.

Never allow a situation to go really sour. Whatever may have been done or said, you have to go on working with that pupil for a year or even more. You must therefore firmly resist using words that you cannot recant and which leave you in a posture of irrevocable anger and dislike. You can criticize what he has *done* or *said* or *not done* as strongly as you like (although temperateness is advisable), but you must not venture from his crimes to himself. You must not criticize *him*. Too often I have come across situations where the teacher has allowed his justifiable indignation at an unpleasant action of a pupil to lead him into a bitter attack on the over-all character of the pupil. I submit that this is unjustified, as the teacher's current task is to define and criticize the action only, and, closer to my present point, it is unwise, as it puts the relationship in a position from which it can never recover. If you put a pupil beyond the pale you are preventing all hope of future communication. Yesterday's action can be forgiven and forgotten, as can yesterday's criticism of it. But yesterday's character assassination has a continuing life, is still significant today, and will be remembered bitterly.

There are some unfair tactics that teachers slip into in the heat of the moment. You may feel that you will never indulge in such unpleasantness, but it is worth being warned so that you can see the temptation coming, and steer away:

Never refer to a pupil's family in front of other pupils. Never use the ill fame of other brothers and sisters, perhaps because they were at the school, to criticize a pupil. Never make invidious comparisons with other members of the family.
Never say anything to wound.
Never refer to physical or racial characteristics.

There will sometimes be disobedience from all classes and with all teachers. It is essential to take up the first instance and calmly, fairly, but firmly, prevent it and punish it. It is far better for all concerned to act on that first instance, however small, rather than to wait until you have to impose unjust, wholesale punishment on the whole of an unruly class. (By the way, always keep the first fortnight at a new school clear, especially of after-school engagements: you must be free to take immediate action on those first few defaulters right at the start.) American research into classroom behaviour[1] certainly supports the common-sense realization that there are techniques of stopping trouble, and that some teachers are more successful than others, not because of their fierceness or punitiveness, but because of their skill. The researchers in that study scored hundreds of hours of video-taped lessons according to the ability the teacher had to stop misbehaviour. They invented the term 'withitness', which rather nicely describes the ability of a teacher to communicate to the pupils that he or she knows what's going on. If a teacher can communicate that fact to the class, without necessarily having to declare it aloud, much of the potential trouble will never take place. The teachers who have become immersed in helping an individual, or stopping one bit of trouble, often pick the wrong pupil, especially picking on an appreciative onlooker or an imitative pupil rather than the initiator. They also frequently object to a less serious deviancy, and overlook a more serious fault that is taking place at the same time or has taken place between the last reprimand and this. Timing mistakes are sometimes the fault of a teacher's being engrossed in other matters, but they are also often the result of a teacher's being anxious not to appear too strict.

[1] Kounin, Jacob S., *Discipline and Classroom Management*, Holt, Rinehart and Winston, Inc., 1970.

For instance, if two children start to whisper, when the class should be listening to another pupil reading aloud, and a third joins them, it is a mistake of timing to wait until the third starts before reprimanding the whisperers. Similarly it is a timing mistake to wait until bad behaviour has increased in seriousness before stopping it. Minor irritations of one pupil by another are frequent examples of this error in timing. One pupil pushed another's head lightly as he passed back to his seat. The second pupil then turned and dug the first pupil in the back. At that the first pupil really hit the second – and only then did the teacher consider it serious enough to reprimand him. I have found that very many of the serious incidents in classrooms that teachers can't deal with arise out of initial errors in picking the wrong person or picking the wrong timing for the reprimand. Further, in almost all cases the teacher's error has been to leave the situation too long, thus reprimanding the second rather than the first pupil misbehaving, or the victim rather than the aggressor. In errors of target the teacher produces resentment as well as failing to stop the bad behaviour. In errors of timing it could be said that the teacher almost encourages the worse behaviour by not noticing the early stages.

If at any time you find that there is a serious situation beyond your responsibility or power, do not hesitate but immediately use whatever method the school has for gathering support. If a pupil, for instance, is grossly abusive or disobedient, do not be too proud or feel that you will weaken your position by referring the matter to a senior member of staff.[1] A grave breach of discipline does occasionally happen, even with the most consistently successful teachers and even with the most co-operative pupils. You are not helping the pupil, yourself, or the school if you hesitate. The class and the individual must realize that what has happened is intolerable and that you will not tolerate it. Therefore send at once for a senior member of staff (usually in writing), suspend the class activity, and isolate the individual. There is no need for a witch-hunt – the pupil will usually realize that retribution and apology are required. But don't hesitate.

---

[1] In a well-organized school it will have been made clear to you precisely whom to call and in what way. It is obviously important that the school defines roles and lines of communication clearly, and that senior staff do indeed support their less experienced colleagues.

Physical Action

I am not here concerned with the wider argument about the use
of corporal punishment, but merely with how the individual
teacher can best cope in the classroom, whatever the regula-
tions and atmosphere of the school in which he works. There
are going to be occasions when you are tempted to hit a pupil,
or otherwise use some form of physical punishment. Don't.
However slight your action, it will do more harm than good.
This includes supposedly jocular acts like hair-pulling or
ear twisting: It has been well said in the past: 'Never touch
a pupil in anger or affection.'

Young people deeply resent any form of physical molesta-
tion. Boys are much more likely to accept the formally inflicted
cane than a cuff round the ear, or a swipe at the backside. It is
difficult to capture in words the deep sense of personal affront
which any such action creates in most pupils. Although this
is a general reaction, it is especially deeply held by girls, who
have an acute sense of their physical growth and dignity from
an early age.

There is no halfway house. Teachers occasionally seize a
pupil's collar, thinking that this is not true physical assault.
It feels it to the pupil. Furthermore, there are no nice distinctions. It is impossible in retrospect to work out exactly when
you touched and what happened. If the pupil thinks the teacher
used more force than he actually did, the harm to the relationship has been done.

You will notice that I have discussed this entirely in terms of
the theme of this chapter – relationships in the classroom. That
is the main reason why you should refrain from all physical
punishment. In addition, however, I should remind you that to
assault a pupil in any way is to lay yourself open to the possibility of prosecution by parents and a slur on your professional record.

All that having been said, I must add that we are all human
and tempers can be lost. There are very few teachers who have
not struck a pupil at some time or other in their career. A time
will come when either you are in a particularly touchy state
or a pupil is extremely irritating, and you strike out. Should
this happen, don't cover it up. Send at once for a senior
member of staff. If one is not available, go to see your Head
of Department or the Deputy Head as soon as the lesson is
over.

Humour

A joke goes a long way. Try to be light-hearted whenever you feel up to it. Try to chivvy recalcitrant pupils jokingly rather than by being indignant. 'Rule by quip' one Headmaster called it. Be willing to make jokes at your own expense, and to laugh at your own foibles. Teachers' jokes don't have to be very good to be nevertheless highly acceptable. I have noticed that some young teachers with high ideals and considerable theoretical understanding of 'under-privileged' children take themselves, their responsibilities, and their pupils too solemnly. Their humourless indignation and sad intensity alienates their charges. I am not recommending a continuous bonanza of laughter, and certainly pupils can get tired of constant hearty jokes or tireless facetiousness. In general, though, try to be bright and modestly 'jokey'.

If you do or say anything that inadvertently makes the children laugh at you, accept the situation rapidly and grace-fully. If possible, make some remark that acknowledges you have made a comic slip, join the laughter for a moment, and then quickly pick up the thread of the lesson, and reinstate the usual atmosphere. The aim is to accept the situation and share the humour, but not to indulge yourself or them. You won't succeed in teaching if you are taken as a clown, but neither will you if you are humourless and so much on your dignity that you can't accept the pupils' laughter. Take a joke at your own expense, but don't exploit it.

Conclusion

In many ways it is lonely to be a teacher. Whatever happens, however you try, whatever intimacy you create, you will remain an adult and a teacher; your charges will remain young and pupils. It is tempting but a delusion to try to remove the bar-riers. This is true even in the closest situations in out-of-school activities. It is doubly so in the classroom itself. There are suitable conventions of reticence. It may well be that you will occasionally want to reveal various details of your out-of-school life, but you should take care. Not only does a teacher need and deserve a private life, but once you break the normal boundary control there is no reasonable way of re-establishing it when it suits you. The conventions of a certain school-teacherly distance are not the creation of proud or cold people.

Rather they are the practical necessities for human contact in a continuing *professional* relationship. After all, the pupils are not of your family, and there is nothing you can do to make them so. Even if they were, there are still barriers that are mutually accepted and mutually valuable in a family. It is worth remembering how difficult parents usually find it to teach their own children. The teaching relationship can flourish precisely because it does not have the full intimacy, with all the tension that involves, of a family. A teacher must keep behind his barriers precisely *for the sake of the relationships.*

A final word: the better things go, the better relationships will be; and then the better the lessons will go. It is the teacher's responsibility to start up this 'virtuous circle', and his best step is to make sure as far as possible that pupils keep out of trouble in the classroom. Pupils like teachers who help them to their better selves; they dislike teachers who generate situations in which the pupils show the worst side of themselves. Run a calm, well-ordered, active classroom, in which no one is allowed to go far wrong, and you will be rewarded by growing good relationships.

3 The Classroom Environment

You are lucky if you are going to have a classroom of your
own. Push for it if you can, and make the most of it if you have
one. A room of your own means that you can create an atmosphere that reflects your character and what you have to offer
the pupils who come to you; it allows you to use wall displays
as teaching aids; it means that you can manage the practical
supply of learning materials better, have the pupils' work easily
to hand, and never have to search for anything; it means, above
all, that you can use the physical environment of the room as
an ally in influencing your pupils. Thus effort taken in the care,
arrangement, and maintenance of your room, especially if you
enlist the help of a small number of pupils, is a valuable investment that will repay rich dividends. Put simply, not only is
a well-kept and aesthetically pleasing room with functional displays an education in itself, but also pupils behave better in
a room which is well organized and has individual character.

The general impression which the pupil has of the room
starts with the door. If there is space for a name card, and it is
left to you to prepare it, do so with care, using Letraset[1] if you
are not a good calligrapher. If there is a window, it is best left
clear, but if you are going to mount the name of your class,
do so boldly, neatly, and in such a position that it is still easy
to see through the window.

Opening the door, the pupil's first impression is of the layout
of the desks. There is something infinitely depressing about a
scatter of desks and chairs with no recognizable pattern, chairs
in aisles, desks at all angles. I discuss possible layouts a little
later (page 27), but I must stress the value of pleasing tidiness
as the first impression a pupil receives.

He often notices the blackboard second. Is it clean? Has
it carefully prepared work on it? Or does it still bear smudged
traces of earlier lessons, or, worse still, pupils' playful scrawls?
I discuss the use of the blackboard in chapter 6. I would add

[1] Available from most large art suppliers, or catalogue from Letraset Ltd,
195 Waterloo Road, London, SE1.

here, though, that it is boldly there to see as pupils come through the door, and it flies like an advertising flag across one side of the room, declaring it as a room of work or a room of chaos at a moment's glance.

Next, it is the general cleanliness and tidiness of the room which strikes the incoming pupil. He may not comment; he may only be half consciously aware, but he will notice the floor, the ledges and the desks. It will affect his attitude and behaviour if they are messy and if there is litter about. Make sure that the room is always tidy. Each class should be asked to clear up thoroughly before it leaves, and at the end of the day the last class should give the room a final checkover. Each pupil should be responsible for his or her area, including any neighbouring shelves or ledges, and any shelves or lockers which are part of the desk. Don't allow reservoirs of litter to build up anywhere, especially under desks: it all spills out later. Make sure that your sections of the room are similarly neat. Keep any piles of used books neatly and use book-ends to keep your own books orderly. Teachers frequently amass miscellaneous piles of virtually abandoned books to gather chalk dust near the blackboard. Ruthlessly clear and chuck regularly. In a busy teaching day you cannot afford to be confused by clutter.

Early on, get to know the cleaner responsible for your room. She deserves the thoughtfulness of your care, and you need her help. In most schools, chairs are put up on to desks to help the cleaners. I think it appropriate that pupils should consider who cleans up after them, and should contribute their amount of help at least. If you are punctilious about this help, and make sure that there is no litter on the floor, the cleaner is more likely to co-operate with you.

There is bound to be damage from time to time – chair backs, window catches, blinds. Be sure you know the maintenance procedures in your school. To whom should you report damage to the fabric or furniture? Report any damage *at once*, and gently enquire about progress. Arrange for graffiti to be removed immediately. Any breakages or signs of abuse are invitations to further damage. The longer a piece of damage is left on public view, the more it contributes to the general acceptance of breakage. Anyone who has seen a heavily vandalized school will be appalled by the atmosphere of degradation. Some rooms in otherwise fairly well-kept schools also become like that. The effect on pupils of such surroundings is depressing. I strongly recommend careful efforts to maintain your room in first-rate order.

As the pupil actually moves across the room, the effect of any display boards will strike him, and it is these that will be in the outskirts of his vision throughout his time in the room. They form, with windows and blackboards, two of his learning boundaries. They are important. Most classrooms have display boards and it is wise to make good use of them. Blank boards are grey and dismal; messy boards, with the scars of past graffiti or the flaunting challenge of live graffiti, are a spur to discontent and bad behaviour. For those reasons alone, it is worth devising and maintaining lively, changing displays. More positively, however, the boards can be an active part of the teaching in a variety of ways.

I find it easier if I roughly divide the board areas out in advance so that I can estimate approximately how often changes are required, and how much material is necessary. Have one well-kept section for the school's standing notices, whatever they may be: fire drill, lesson times, list of teachers, etc. As these will have to stay up for a whole year, they must be well pinned, preferably mounted and covered with a transparent sealing material.[1]

Secondly, keep a small section for your own form or tutor group to display their personal, perhaps quirkish, interests: cuttings, pieces of writing, photographs, etc.

You can then have a main central display section for some aspect of your subject which is of general interest. This should not be changed too often – you won't be able to manage it and the pupils won't have taken it in. Nor should it be left up for too long, or it will fade and go stale. A half-termly cycle seems about right, and that requires six in a year. (Have the first one ready *before* term starts, by the way.) The materials for small displays can come from educational publishers, commercial posters, free handouts, press clippings, magazines, and specially prepared diagrams.

Lastly, you can mark off sections for displays of written work by each of your classes. Normally these should be 'fair copies' especially prepared for display, but you may at times prefer to use first drafts. Ensure a cross-section of examples and a reasonably frequent changeover. Again, use careful display techniques.

In all four types of display, a firm grid pattern helps, and good quality labels add a great deal. Those which are likely to

[1] There is an excellent account of simple display techniques in Robert Leggat's *Showing off*. See book list on page 101.

stand for a long time should be well prepared and protected. Finally, don't forget to *use* the displays: they can be referred to during lessons; the final minutes of a session can be given over to questions and answers in connection with them; or a class can be sent in groups to do a worksheet based on a display. Thus the displays make the room more personally the teacher's, they add colour and interest, they have an educational function, and they show you care. They are worth the trouble.

Some teachers cultivate simple pot plants on window-sills or shelves. (The success of this nicety usually depends on the willingness of the caretaking or cleaning staff to water in the holidays!) Such a pleasantness is appreciated by most pupils. The touch of colour and natural life softens the classroom, and increases pride. Of course, pupils from your own class can help with the maintenance. Other personally chosen objects or pictures to your taste can also be imported, and increase the extent of your personal touch.

Part of the aim, then, is to encourage the pupils to feel that even though they visit the room only a few times in the week, they share in the care of it. Unlike what is possible in a Junior school, most Middle schools, and the first year of some Secondary schools, the typical Secondary pattern of classes moving to teachers does not allow the full identification of pupils with 'their' room. It has, instead, to be replaced by the feeling of visiting a teacher's 'own' room. So make the room yours as completely as you can. Make it welcoming, interesting, cheerful, and workmanlike. You can make the room itself an ally of your control.

Layout and Seating

The position of the teacher's desk is worth thought. Except in many science labs, the dais has been removed from almost all rooms, and the dominant raised front-centre position abandoned. Young teachers hoping for a close rapport with their pupils tend to search for less and less dominating positions, perhaps shifting the desk to one side of the front, and then even down the side. I should suggest that for most purposes a front side position is probably best. The desk must be so positioned that:

a. all the pupils can see the teacher when he or she is at the desk;
b. the desk is clearly visible from the door.

Even in a relaxed modern classroom atmosphere and even in an individual research kind of lesson, the focal presence of the teacher is important. In a busy classroom you will see pupils' eyes flick up to where they expect to see the teacher. Some of the looks will be from pupils wondering momentarily whether to do something silly or not. Others will be from pupils who are deep in their work but want some kind of reassurance. The stable figure of the teacher in a known position in the room is a comforting influence. This position, therefore, does need to be a focal point.

Secondly, your desk will be where you lay out what *you* need for the lesson time. Spare paper for the pupils can be in a position convenient for their movement to it, but your books, class list, notes, pens, handbag, and anything you might want whilst talking to the class or helping an individual must be conveniently laid out. The teacher's desk is normally the best place for all this, and so it must be near your normal focal position. I have seen teachers placing their desk in an out-of-the-way position, and then finding that they have difficulty dodging back and forth.

Thirdly, if you wish to give a great deal of individual care you will probably find this done best at your own desk, with a pupil sitting to one side. (I find this immensely more effective than dodging about the room, crouching or bending to help individuals, as I describe later on pages 64–65.) This means, again, that your desk must be placed in a focal position, so that you can still influence the room whilst helping individuals, that there must be sufficient space by your desk for a pupil's chair, and that there must be reasonably easy access to and from the desk.

For all these reasons I am much happier in a room where I have a desk or table which is easy to get at and round, is adjacent to the best focal position for board work and questions, and is in a pleasant focal position for when I am quietly helping an individual pupil.

Next, consider the pupils' tables or desks. How do you want these laid out? There is rarely an ideal layout in a normal-sized classroom, but the search for an optimum layout is worth while. The basic difficulty is so to arrange the furniture that each pupil can have both the degree of privacy necessary for the majority of work, and the possibility of co-operative groupings at other times. A second difficulty is to arrange the desks so that each pupil has as much space as possible, and yet to allow sufficient space for movement around the class. Equal spacing, for instance, suits the first aim, and each pupil has the maximum elbow room. However, by losing all the circulation space, congestion is created when the teacher or a pupil needs to move around the room. Circulation space must be kept, and it is often forgotten that if there is to be a great deal of individual work it is even more important: SMP cards, SRA reading cards, and the glut of individual assignment cards now available to schools all presume a steady flow of pupils moving to pick up the next card, check a completed card, or gather new materials. The regulation aisles, which usually have no cross connection without pushing against chair backs, are inadequate.[1]

Careful thought should be given in advance to what line you are going to take about the pupils' regular positions at desks, tables, lab benches, or other work-benches. You cannot dither uncertainly as your pupils first arrive, nor can you easily change your mind from lesson to lesson. In particular, it is virtually impossible after a number of sessions in which there has been free pupil choice. The decision must be taken in advance, and must then be kept to for at least a considerable run of time.

The issue is simple to define: are the best interests of the pupils served by allowing them to choose their own normal positions, or is there anything to be gained by your determining the arrangements yourself? Before you rush to one side or the other, it is worth a careful exploration of the often contradictory attitudes that lie behind the arguments on both sides. At first glance it seems more generous, more in tune with encouraging pupil autonomy, and more likely to gain the goodwill of the pupils if you allow them to find their own places. Certainly you would expect sixth-formers to settle their own seating, but how far down the age range would you go? And what characteristic is it that would lead you to make the decision? It is worth remembering the different situations and not merely the different ages: sixth-formers frequently meet in a room with spare seats, for a subject which they have chosen, and in a much smaller group than a younger class. In other words, it is not merely age that should be taken into account but the entire pattern of the activity.

A full class of, say, thirty pupils coming into a room with which they are not familiar and being left to themselves is in-

[1] If you do not have exclusive use of a room, to devise eccentric arrangements is unfair on your colleagues.

teresting to observe. A few come in first and settle in a group by the window; a bunch of three of four dash for the back and ensconce themselves with a defiant air of territorial possession; friends try to keep together; a few nervous children find it difficult to settle as the odd seats apparently left over prove to be reserved for friends. At the end you usually find a quiet boy desperately trying to avoid the only seat, which is in fact next to a large girl, whereas the rest of the class are sexually segregated. As a teacher you find yourself atmospherically excluded from various of the groups which have formed, and you soon realize that you have neither a 'class' nor a series of individuals but a number of factions of different strengths and degrees of unity to contend with.

It could be argued, and frequently is, that this kind of peer-group-determined seating is precisely what is best for the pupils, for it will encourage co-operation and maintain the favourable attitude of the pupils. It is argued further by some who claim a special sympathy with the young that the pupils have a natural 'right' to choose their own seating.

As you will have gathered from my way of phrasing the arguments, I am by no means certain that justice, pleasantness, or learning effectiveness are on the side of allowing the pupils to choose their seating arrangements. In the first place, the teacher must be the leader of the classroom, his will-power must be sufficient to make things work. By making the first set of decisions about seating, he is clearly stating that this is his room, and that things will be run his way. (There will be ample opportunity later for the pupils to exercise their influence.) For the teacher to start the year by organizing the seating is to start as he intends to go on – as the leader.

Secondly, I'm not at all sure that the apparent friendship groups that determine the seating when a free-for-all is allowed are always the most beneficial ones for the pupils. They are more power groups than friendship groups, and are not necessarily appreciated equally throughout the class by all the pupils. As so often happens, the vociferous few may well have their demands met at the expense of the general good. The powerful block that this system allows to flourish almost inevitably draws the teacher's time and care, both in class teaching and individual work, from the remainder of the class. Time and time again I have seen teachers allow, even encourage, such groups to grow in the interest of fairness, freedom, and gaining goodwill, only to find the class as a whole is unmanageable because of the obstreperous caucus which dominates the room and is impossible to satisfy or quieten.

Thirdly, I am not at all sure that 'friends' need each other or are always good for each other in the learning situation. Whatever the class activity – a mixed-ability class coping with worksheets in Humanities, pairs co-operating, or the whole class listening to a presentation – a proportion of your pupils is going to be easily distracted. The distractors will usually be their friends. Some pupils spend so much time in each other's company in homes, street, and playground that they just cannot resist teasing each other, joking, and talking. It is harmless, pleasant, but distracting. There is no hardship in expecting these close friends to work for a double period in other groupings – they get hours of each other's company. It is in no way 'unreal' or 'artificial', for in most jobs they will have to work independently of best friends. Indeed, it is a necessary preparation for all kinds of work to learn to work quietly on your own. It is in fact a truism that some pupils need protecting *from* their friends, so that they can be more genuinely themselves.

Fourthly, 'individualized' teaching requires the teaching of individuals when there is not a real need for a group togetherness. I have found that young teachers commonly stress their wish to teach individuals. Often, however, they allow virtually impenetrable small groups to bring their sealing-off relationships into the classroom. Thus the teacher is unable to develop a truly individual approach to Joan as she is always part of the Siamese twin 'Joan and Lorraine'. Whilst it is certainly true that her closeness to Lorraine is a part of her and to be respected, it is also true that the teacher will never get near to the real Joan until he can prise them apart and get her on her own. Then he will find unexpected sides to her character. Whilst the pair are performing as a pair, only those parts of their characters which overlap are allowed by either of them to surface. The rest is deliberately hidden. Those hidden parts need teaching also, and are often more teachable than the joint features of the 'Joan and Lorraine' pair. It shows no real respect for the individuals Joan and Lorraine to let them remain together, and it tends to deny them both communication with the teacher, and even with the class.

Fifthly, supposedly free choice (it is not, after all, free for all the pupils) almost inevitably leads to arguments in subsequent lessons when two or three pupils have decided to vary their seats; a few others, finding 'their' seats taken, obligingly search out alternatives; and a chain of moves is necessary as the pupils gradually fill the room. Somewhere along the line, however, a pupil sticks, insists on 'his' own place, and refuses the empty seat. At that point there is a ripple of rows that is difficult or impossible for any teacher to sort out. As such an arrangement has invested no especial authority in any particular pattern of seats, and as each period has had some slight variation, there is no clear scheme or agreed precedent to refer to. As the pupils themselves established all the variations, there is no authority to arbitrate. The lesson founders before it starts in a welter of pointless arguing. In the end the teacher finds he is absolutely obliged to dictate some shifts and re-seatings. He has lost the goodwill, wasted time, and has the unenviable task of starting a lesson amongst sulks. The paradox is that the earlier apparent freedom leads to frequent re-impositions of the teacher's will. There is not time in a school day or space in a school classroom for this kind of difficulty.

Finally, there is the teacher's need to know without a moment's thought exactly where each pupil is working. Es-pecially with large classes, this is possible only if each pupil works in precisely the same position period after period. Then the teacher absorbs the pattern into his subconcious, and can turn to a pupil straightaway.

For these six reasons, then, I should strongly recommend that the initial seating of a class is done by the teacher and to a plan devised by him. In a Science laboratory this may involve two sets of positions – those for central explanation and those for individual or small-group activity and experiment. Prepare a sketch plan of the work positions available in your room. Run off a number of copies of this if you like – sufficient for two or so for each of your classes. Then study your class list and what you know of each pupil before deciding on your arrangement. An alphabetical sequence is the obvious arbitrary decision that does not raise any challengeable points. It also has the added practical advantage, for which you will be grateful week after week, that it follows the normal order of registers, school lists, and your own mark book. Notice, however, that even the ap-parently inflexible alphabetical order offers you some helpful variations. If you are teaching in a mixed school, for instance, it is normal to list girls first and then boys. For seating, I per-sonally prefer to produce a single alphabetical list, boys and girls together in their correct alphabetical position. This is not done very commonly, and you may well prefer the more common division into two lists. My personal preference is based on the simple fact that most class misbehaviour results from the interaction of pupils of the same sex. This scheme frequently puts a boy next to a girl. Of course, you can achieve this even more rigorously by interspersing boy/girl with two separate alphabetical sequences, but this makes the listing more complicated, and it lacks the simplicity of explanation to the class.

If you are lucky enough to have slightly fewer pupils in your teaching group than there are actual seats or work-bench spaces in your room, I strongly recommend that you exploit the spare seats as buffers to improve the psychological separation of pupils or groups. It is pointless to allow a block of four empty seats when other sectors of the room are crowded. Instead, distribute the spare seats as you judge best. It might be wise with one class to keep the back row, the trouble-maker's instinctive chair-swinging row, empty. In another class you may distribute the empty seats here and there, merely to thin the seating out. You may use your knowledge of the pupils in another class to decide that Gary or Elaine is best left sitting in isolation. After all, in a great deal of learning activity a psychological barrier between individuals is valuable – I wouldn't want someone nudging me or breathing down my shoulder whilst I was drafting this chapter. You'd find it harder to read the chapter if your best friend were right next to you, constantly asking you to lend your pen, pencil, ruler, etc.

With mixed-ability classes I find planned seating even more important. Implicit in mixed-ability grouping is a fair proportion of individual or small group work. You may occasionally require homogenous sub-grouping, in which case you clearly must organize the groups yourself. You may, on the other hand, want pairs or groups to be mixed also, in which case your influence is equally necessary. Above all, the greater fluidity of mixed-ability teaching implies the need for the control that comes only from controlled seating. The seating plan, then, is a method of assisting the psychological insulation of crowded pupils, and can sometimes be subtly manipulated to separate certain individuals or to leave others entirely on their own.

Have your arrangement decided and noted down in advance. Prepare a sketch plan of the work positions available, and run off one or two blanks for each class. Have one in your hand when you first greet the incoming class. A second copy is useful as the first pupil who arrives can be issued with it and stationed on the far side of the room to help with the directions:

it is much better to get pupils straight to the seats you have chosen, rather than to have to evict them. That does cause resentment. If you feel it is better to seat them rapidly any old how, make the pupils fill the seats up from the front as they come in. Do not let the choosing process start, and then disappoint the early squatters. When the seats are full, go round the desks calling out the names of the permanent tenants, asking each dispossessed pupil to rise and stand at the front until his or her name is called for a seat. You'll find that this method of re-seating works quite well.

Post one copy of the seating plan on the notice board for checking up at the start of the next lesson, and paste the other copy clearly in your class register. You will find this very convenient, as it allows you to identify the pupils by name rapidly. You may also like to have each pupil note the position of his or her desk in a workbook on the first occasion, to help memorize it for the next lesson.

You may feel that I have elaborated the point about seating unnecessarily and neurotically. It is, however, my considered opinion that care over the seating contributes more than any other single piece of initial management to the control of the class in subsequent weeks. I have been through years of trying to work with freer and more relaxed methods. Nowadays, even with the additional help of a Headmaster's status, I should not consider teaching a class regularly without seating the pupils to my own plan. As the weeks go by, I might allow a few changes bit by bit, but the plan is there, establishing our working pattern, and seeing us through those first weeks. Don't be put off by initial face-pulling: the pupils prefer it too!

It would be fair to say that the physical impression of the classroom can be an ally or an enemy in teaching, and part of the art of the classroom is to *use* the room itself. Its arrangement can contribute to the control, the learning, the relationships, and the pleasure of working together.

4 Records, Registers, and Reports

Teachers traditionally despise 'paperwork'. I've never discovered why, as we are always trying to raise our professional status, and pride in an inability to cope with routine administration is hardly likely to do that. Good record-keeping is in fact essential both to the success of an individual teacher's work and to the relationship between his work and that of other colleagues. In these days of rapid staff turn-over, good record-keeping is doubly essential if there is to be continuity of care. But careful paperwork is more than a way of covering over the cracks; it is a positive help towards staff collaboration. To make a record requires an analysis; the process of recording involves the process of assessing. This is helpful. Then to pass the record on, or to gather together records from a number of teachers, is inevitably to prompt a fresh look and often to initiate a programme of collaboration.

Modern methods of teaching require even greater care in record-keeping than older procedures. A mixed-ability group depends on much more careful assessment and record-keeping. Extensive 'project work', with pupils engaged on long pieces of research and writing, flounders in a morass of confusion if the teacher does not keep a record of what each pupil is achieving. In general, you will find your work goes far more satisfactorily if your handling of all the paperwork is adept, unostentatious, and accurate.

Your Mark Book

Don't despise an old-fashioned 'mark book'. In most Authorities each school uses an official issue of a pattern laid down years ago by a long-forgotten decision. The very phrase 'mark book' may smack of a bygone age, of formal cold relationships, and of the rigid teaching of exercises. Don't be misled. It is one of your most vital tools, especially valuable in informal teaching, vital to mixed-ability work, and an aid to your close relationships. And this is so even if you rarely award a numerical 'mark'.

What is commonly called a 'mark book' is in fact your personal, central, portable record system, by which you monitor and record your many pupils' attendance, work, progress, and a wide range of other facts. Do not over-trust your memory. A Secondary teacher may have a case-load of between 150 and 300 pupils for whom he or she is responsible in a particular subject area. No one's memory can hold all that is required for the teaching of so many people without the aid of records. Even Junior-school teachers with many fewer pupils have to use careful records.

Although I would stress that the primary purpose of full records is for the teacher to help himself with his teaching, it is also worth remembering the inevitable absences. If a teacher is away ill and a supply teacher has to take over his lessons, the records are essential. Teachers should ask themselves just how comprehensive and effective their records would be if another teacher tried to continue to teach the classes of the absent teacher.

There are five uses for records:

1. THE LIST OF PUPILS FOR WHOM YOU ARE RESPONSIBLE.   When you are teaching the school's standard registration units ('forms', 'classes', or 'Tutor Groups'), you will normally take these lists off the school's master lists. If, on the other hand, you are teaching 'sets' (that is, groupings formulated only for the one subject), you must get these lists from your Head of Department. Either way, be accurate in transferring the names to your records, and let the pupils know clearly that you have such a list. (Do not accept into your class pupils who are not on your list! In large schools obliging teachers have been known to accept pupils who turned up to a lesson, and to put their names at the foot of the list. Weeks later it is discovered that these pupils ought to be somewhere else!)

Leave space alongside each pupil's name for such basic information as the name of his Tutor (if yours is a mixed set), medical information, etc. It is worth leaving a few vertical columns blank alongside the list of names.

2. ATTENDANCE AT LESSONS.   It is an absolute obligation to check during each lesson which pupils are present and which are absent from your room. It is easiest if you date the head of each column so that there is a column for each session that you will meet in the term. If you put a heavier rule after each

week's columns it will be easier to find your place. This kind of advance preparation of the mark book is amply repaid by the time saved when you are actually in the classroom coping with the pupils. It is hopeless if you try to write in names *then*, and even heading columns wastes time.

Some time during each lesson, enter those present and absent. It is not necessary, nor is it normally wise, to actually 'call' the register aloud. It is certainly not a good practice to do so at the start of a lesson, as this requires you to hold the attention of the class and control their behaviour for a list of names, an unnecessarily difficult job. However, it is most important that the pupils know that you do check the attendance carefully and regularly, for there is plenty of evidence that in areas where truancy is attractive and fairly common, pupils absent themselves not so much from teachers or lessons they do not like as teachers who they know do not make careful checks. Thus in the early days the list of names should be called aloud, whilst the pupils are working, and throughout the year you should demonstrate that you are checking regularly.

Each school will have its own procedures to help you ascertain whether those absent from your lesson are genuinely absent from school or not. In some schools you will be expected to check with lists of absentees posted on a central notice board; in others, you will have to check personally with the main class register; and in others, there will be routine chits that you are expected to fill up and send to the Head of Year, Head of House, or office. Be punctilious about these procedures, and *let the pupils know that you do this checking as a matter of course.*

3. RECORDS OF WORK COMPLETED. You must know what your pupils have accomplished. Some Junior-school teachers, who are responsible for virtually the whole of a pupil's learning, note specific aspects of, for example, reading, in elaborate records. I have come to the conclusion that some such record-keeping is essential. Even in the continuous and intimate relationship of the Junior-school classroom, it is obvious that a pupil can slip through the teacher's mind without it registering that a certain activity or learning skill has constantly eluded that particular pupil.

Each subject in the Secondary school will require a slightly different recording system, but basically the teacher needs to note each step or item of work completed. When the entire class is expected to do each exercise or piece of writing simultaneously, and to finish on the same occasion, the recording of this is fairly easy. It is worth noting that this work pattern is still very common, and is likely to remain so. Even in a mixed-ability class, items of work are normally done in sequence. There are two basic ways of recording the items of work done: the vertical column can identify the *dates* of the work sessions, in class or at home if all the pupils are doing the same piece of work; the horizontal line against the pupil's name indicates satisfactory completion by a tick, or can be used for a grade or 'mark'. If the pupils are working on different assignments, such as different stages of a work-card scheme or different self-chosen pieces of writing, the horizontal line indicates briefly the title or number of the piece of work. Obviously, in this case, a greater horizontal width is required, and two or three vertical columns are best used for each session. Alternatively, if the pupils are expected to work methodically, but at their own individual paces, through a sequence of assignments, the *vertical* columns can be used to identify the assignments, and the pupils' horizontal lines the dates on which each assignment is completed. Grades can easily be incorporated into this dating system.

There is an obvious need to join together the second function – attendance – with this third function – work completed. With the number of classes and the normal pattern of a Secondary timetable, you will find it impossible to remember with certainty who completed what when. I have heard interminable arguments between a well-meaning teacher and devious pupils about whether a piece of work from a week or two back should have been done or not:

'But I was absent, Miss.'
'Not on the day we did that piece of work.'
'Yes, I was. Don't you remember, Miss, 'cos when I came back . . . . '

And so it goes on. Your records need to be clear enough to avoid all arguments. One possible method is to use separate pages for work had attendance. In that case you need to check back when there is doubt. Alternatively, you can put the pupils' names only on *every other* horizontal line, using the first horizontal line for absent/present signs, and the second one for work records, thus:

	10 Sept	12 Sept	14 Sept	17 Sept	19 Sept	21 Sept
CLODETH BROWN	A	√	√	√	√	√
		8	5		6	4
LORRAINE CLARKE	√	√	A	A	√	√
	4	5			3	3
JOAN DARBY		√	√	√	√	√
	6	6	7		7	8

. . . .
. . . .

| Exercise 3 | Hint Ex 7 Diagrams | | Test | Exercise 10 |

Either way, I recommend a clear code system to remind you of the work situation. For every work session when something should have been committed to paper (whether a homework session or a class session), there are five possibilities. I recommend that you decide on a sign for each square in your mark book that will later tell you immediately and unambiguously what happened. You will find this most helpful when you read through the pupils' work at home later, and when you hand it back:

The pupil hands in completed work
(leaving space for grade later):   √

The pupil was absent, and did not do the work: A

The pupil was absent when the work should have been
handed in, but not when it should have been actually
done (this especially applies to homework)
(again, space left for grade later):   a

The pupil did not hand anything in, and chasing
therefore needed: •

The pupil present and worked, but did not complete,
and you have agreed to more time: −

Obviously there are innumerable variations in ways of using a gridded mark book to keep tabs on the flow of work. Be clear, consistent, and careful, and you will remove almost all the classroom arguments that sour relationships and take time. Vague teachers somehow think such records are anti-creative. They are in fact the servants of caring teaching.

4. RECORDS OF BOOKS ISSUED.   In a later section (on page 54) I discuss ways of handing out books, apparatus, and work-sheets for a single lesson. Books issued to be taken from the room, however, must be recorded, and this is a further function of the 'mark' book.

Most subjects use sets of printed books at least some of the time; indeed, for all the emphasis on other kinds of resources, many subjects depend on every pupil having a book to hand. The teacher must establish a routine which is as helpful as pos-sible in making sure that there is no confusion over these books. Their handling can be divided into two categories: books issued for a single session only, and books issued for the pupil to take away for a short or long period. The first category can be thought of in exactly the same way as apparatus and equipment issued for use during a period, and I shall therefore give advice in the section on page 54. Books to be taken away, how-ever, require a different approach. It must be simple, and must be carried out precisely and briskly.

Your school or department may well have a system. If so, you will obviously use it. If not, I recommend the following:

Make sure in advance that the set of books is clearly serial-numbered from one upwards. This is best done with a speci-ally prepared rubber stamp, and many departments prepare these:

Sir Henry Wood School
Golder Grove, Colchester
HISTORY DEPARTMENT
Set No: A4
Copy Number: 5

(Other departments have very large rubber numbered stamps that can be applied to the top of the page edges of the closed book. I find this a less satisfactory method on its own, but it is very clear in a pile of books. If no provision has been made for you, simply number each copy boldly and firmly, perhaps in a coloured ink, in precisely the same place in each copy, perhaps the bottom right-hand corner of the front inside cover. Tell the pupils clearly that each copy is numbered and that you will be keeping a record of the number of each copy in your class list, so that you will know exactly who has which copy. I recommend that, if possible, you actually issue the copies whilst the class are busy with some other work. Do not go round with the full pile of books first, and then gather the numbers. Call each pupil to you one by one (or visit each pupil's desk), hand over the copy personally, show the number, and let the pupil see that it is entered in the list against his or her name. In addition, of course, each pupil should write his or her name neatly and clearly in the copy, using the official school label if there is one.

It is difficult for pupils to remember an irregular require-ment for bringing books to lessons, and spontaneous decisions like 'Oh . . . and I'd like you to bring your atlas to tomorrow's lesson' are almost always a failure: some don't hear, many for-get, a few who come tomorrow are away today, and others have lost their atlas because you use it so rarely. The regular bringing of a clearly stated number of books is easier for all. (If there is a book you use only rarely, then you may prefer to issue it, as discussed on page 51, only for the necessary periods.) Insist on this routine, and make a fuss about it in the early weeks. Keep the Form Master or Tutor informed of any failures. Build up the habit and give lavish praise when it is established. It is perfectly reasonable that your lesson should depend on books: only the creation of a routine will ensure that the majority bring them.

5. COMMENTS ON THE PUPILS.   You should certainly exercise the focusing discipline of going through your class lists once a term and asking yourself how each pupil has been getting on, and recording a comment. This may be required for external reports, or for internal records. If not, do it for your own benefit. Either way, the mark book is an easy place, al-though you may prefer to use a sheet of paper in the pupil's folder, which I mention on page 51. If you use the mark book, I should allow a full double-page spread, cut back so that it aligns with your pupil list.

Before we leave mark *books*, it is worth mentioning that although the single book, which has now become the store-house for so much information about each of your pupils, is very convenient indeed, there are other possible formats. I like to take a manilla double-pocket folder for a single class,

and staple into the centre sufficient gridded mark-book pages
for the class. I can then keep the pupils' current work or file
paper in one pocket, and examples of work sheets, etc. in the
other. I therefore have a compendium for the class with everything that I need in it.

Attendance Registers

Although the formal attendance register is of especial importance, both as a diagnostic tool and as a legal document (which
may have to be produced as evidence in the case of a truancy
prosecution), I shall say less about it than I have said about the
teaching mark book, as most Local Education Authorities print
specific instructions and many schools supplement these with
careful briefings of their own. If you have pastoral responsibility as a Tutor or Form Teacher, you must see the formal
attendance register not as some piece of routine bureaucracy
but as a useful way of helping you to help the pupils and their
families. In the first place, you must know who is and is not
in school, and the school must inform the parents of any
absences by whatever convenient but certain procedure it has
devised. This is not only a legal necessity but a professional
duty: the parent who has seen the child off to school must be
informed if he or she has not arrived. Secondly, the register
is used as a clear record of all notes about absences, dental
appointment cards, and the like received about pupils, and all
information notes about attendance sent to the parents. In
many, perhaps most, cases this information serves merely as
a running check that you have indeed received the necessary ex-
planatory notes. In cases of difficulty, however, you will find
that meticulous record-keeping proves invaluable time and
again when the problem is being reviewed, either by you as
Form Teacher or by senior pastoral staff. When the school staff
need to talk over attendance problems with parents, the
existence of an accurate register, with details of notes and action
taken, is vital.

Thirdly, the same is true of lateness. The normal procedure is
to make a circle if the pupil is not present at the official registration time, and insert an 'L' if he or she arrives later. You should
regard lateness as an aspect of attendance. The register needs
to be accurate, parents need to be informed, and action taken
must be noted.

The fourth point about the register is that, if used sensitively and carefully, it is a remarkably effective diagnostic device. You can see if worrying patterns are building up. Look out for the pattern of absence: the odd half-days are the most worrying. When do they come? Is there any consistent pattern that relates to the time of the week (e.g. Monday a.m., Friday p.m.), or the lesson timetable (does Mary tend to miss Maths?), or other pupils' absences (are two boys truanting together?)? Study your register weekly and look *back* over the year for each pupil. Always make sure parents know of *every* absence or lateness, but also watch if the incidence of either is above average or abnormally patterned. You may then spot difficulties at home, at school, or within the pupil.

Internal Notes

Throughout your teaching there will be a need to inform or consult colleagues about the pupils whom you teach. Perhaps in a small school, especially one organized on Middle-school lines, with a 'class teacher' largely responsible for the work of one group of pupils, it is possible to hold all the needs for communication in your head. In most schools, though, notes are necessary. They also have the advantage of being able to be filed if necessary, and they allow the recipient to consider the matter you have raised at his or her leisure. There is little more infuriating in a large school than a stream of corridor remarks in which, between your classroom and the staffroom cup of tea, three or four teachers throw out important tit-bits of information, most of which you promptly forget to act on, as no mind can take in that kind of barrage.

It is a good idea to have a note-pad always with your mark book, or a supply of slips inside it, so that you can write out notes or queries to colleagues as the points come to you in your lesson, and you can then post them in staffroom pigeon-holes at the end of the session. I am not suggesting that paperwork can be or should be a substitute for personal discussion, but I am stressing that you will *never* have all the conversations about your pupils that you would like, and that you should therefore be willing to use notes as a starting point.

Reports

A less frequent concern than the other points in this chapter will be the writing of reports home to parents. The school report has had a good knock from critics in recent years, and by and large the skimpy, vague, and unhelpful jottings on the blank grids of most reports have justified this. However, the answer is certainly not to abolish reports, but to improve their usefulness. Extensions of opportunities to meet with parents are indeed valuable, but no transient, easily misunderstood conversation is a substitute for a clear, written report. This is a book on the art of the *classroom*, and I cannot devote extensive space to the school report. However, it is an extension of your work in the classroom, and the results will feed back into the classroom. Therefore, I shall give the following brief advice:[1]

Assess each pupil's work with the aid of your mark book before drafting the actual comment.

Thoroughly master the implications and details of any school grading system that your school uses before you put grades into the report forms. It is remarkably easy for new teachers to misunderstand these.

Be positive and helpful.

Be specific and precise, noting actual aspects of work that are going well or need attention.

Be accurate: that is, do not slide over serious problems of behaviour or understanding.

Keep a copy of your comments and grades for your own records and use in discussions with parents and Tutors.

[1] I have written more fully on reporting systems and report comments in chapter 9 of *Pastoral Care*, Heinemann Educational Books, 1974.

5 Conventions and Routines

Every kind of room, from a pub bar to a railway compartment, from a cinema to a snack bar, has to have its own conventions of control if the central activity is to take place at all, and if the people in it are to manage not to offend or interfere with one another. In a public room with a person-to-floor-space density of $8\frac{1}{2}$ square feet per person, one door of $3'$ $6''$ wide, much necessary furniture, and books and papers galore, a set of well-understood conventions is essential for everyone's benefit. Furthermore, pupils are compelled by law to come to school and the least we can do is to create a situation in which each pupil feels that time has been profitably spent. This involves creating a set of conventions for the classroom that are, in very many ways, different from those of the home. The teacher is responsible for creating and sustaining these, and he must not feel hesitant about doing so. The conventions have to be embodied in classroom routines. A convention is a way of economizing on decision-making energy. Just as the conventional greeting of 'Good morning!' avoids the need to think up a form of words to initiate each conversation, so conventions of classroom action avoid dozens of daily decisions and allow real relationships to flourish and the business of learning to go on. Some conventions may not look too sturdy when examined in other lights and on other occasions; nevertheless, they may be immensely valuable in their place. All this is to argue for the value of classroom routines, for they assist class management, permit the growth of close relationships, and allow learning to continue.

Receiving the Class

The majority of Secondary teachers are based in their own rooms for most of their teaching time. I have spoken in chapter 3 of the value of maintaining your room pleasantly and efficiently. I gave there a number of reasons for this: one of them, of course, is the psychological value of receiving the pupils into your territory and a place which is not merely an institutional convenience. However, whether it is your room or just one you use for a particular session each week, the following advice applies.

Be in the room first if at all possible. Unpack and lay out your personal papers and books rapidly and neatly, so that when the pupils have arrived, anything you want is to hand, and you do not have to dive into your bag or fumble through a pile of belongings. Check quickly that the room is in order, the board clean, chalk ready, and any necessary worksheets or books are there. This preliminary early settling in is very helpful. Try very hard to fit it in, even if it means leaving the staffroom chat a little earlier than the old hands. It will be worth it to be first in the room.

Where should you be when the first pupils arrive? Well, obviously there is no one correct place. However, do not be lost in the far corner or tangled in a stock cupboard. Be seen to be the receiving host, as it were. Be in a focal point to encourage the first pupils to go straight to their first activity. Centre-front is clearly one very good position. My own preference, however, is to stand in the doorway, back against the door jamb, facing down the classroom, and at the same time down the corridor outside. (If most teachers were thus positioned at their doors, many of the problems of noisy corridors would be solved.) In this position you can greet each pupil or bunch of pupils as they arrive, and direct them to their first activity. As each passes you, it is possible to put in a personal word to many of them. Private jokes, reminders, enquiries, warnings, encouragement, can all be easily fitted in. You have combined efficient supervision with warm personal relationships. Naturally, you will not want to be nailed to that door jamb for life, but you will find it about the best reception position.

The Start of a Lesson

Every moment of transition in the school day generates inevitable tension and so is a possible source of trouble. Probably the most difficult of these moments is the arrival of a class, and probably the hardest of a Secondary teacher's jobs is the settling down of a class at the start of a new lesson. The stability of the Junior school means that the return from play-time or dinner is often a matter of picking up the earlier threads. The home classroom and the class teacher are there session after session. A Secondary teacher can meet as many as six or even seven different classes in a day (although many schools are now time-tabling for fewer sessions, either by having longer periods or by pairing many of them into doubles). This series of confrontations is one of the most exhausting aspects of the teacher's day, as it requires the rapid adjustment to a different set of personalities, and also requires each time the nervous energy to 'get things going'. Too many young teachers are in fact defeated in the first five minutes as they wait for the class to come in. Whilst waiting for the late-comers, the teacher engages an individual pupil in conversation or sorts out some books. During this gap the rest of the class are building up a crescendo of chatter; some start moving round the room; one or two start an argument; another idly flicks a few pellets. At this stage the teacher decides that all who are coming have arrived, and tries to quell the noise. Just as his voice is being heard with a 'Will you please be quiet' for the third time, two even later late-comers burst through the door. Finding the right words for them would have been difficult anyway, but now the teacher has a double disadvantage. He is flustered from trying to quell the noise and, secondly, his dealing with the late-comers is in front of a gawping class who have nothing to do but watch the telling off. This unconsciously leads the late-comers to play to the gallery, and the teacher to feel that he is in a contest, with the class as umpires – except they are not neutral. If he is wise, he sends them straight to their seats (he's in real trouble if they prove to have been taken and a fresh argument bursts) and starts the lesson. But by now he is working in a difficult atmosphere and he himself is tense. Only a supreme effort of will, voice, and personality can move from this situation into a satisfactory lesson.

What I have described is no 'blackboard jungle', nor does it imply an especially difficult class. I have not exaggerated or pictured an unusually bad situation. These minor difficulties happen daily and they leave the young teacher barely able to cope with the subsequent lesson. He ends the day tired, disappointed, and faintly puzzled at 'what went wrong'. You will notice that the difficulty has nothing to do with curricular planning, pupil grouping, or the preparation of teaching material. It is a matter of class management, and the answer for virtually every subject, every age, and every type of pupil grouping is simple: *have something for every pupil to do when they first enter the room.* Do not expect them to wait for each other or for you, do not have to *call* them to order, don't let them get out of order in the first place.

I describe in chapter 7 the importance of the rhythm of the lesson and analyse possible sequences. Here I am concerned only with the routine of the initial phase. There can be some significant activity on which each pupil can make an immediate start as soon as he comes into the room and without waiting for anyone else. The simplest, where it fits, is for the pupil to be told: 'Spend five minutes looking over last night's homework.' If possible, make the task more specific by focusing the task of checking on one or two elements, e.g.:

'Check the calculation.'
'Make sure you have a good final paragraph.'
'Look especially at the verbs.'

or whatever may be appropriate. A further routine task is to look over a specified paragraph or page in the textbook, in which case the precise reference and the particular object for the task (e.g. 'And find the reasons for . . .') should again be on the board in the expected section. Even simpler still, the pupils may be continuing with whatever piece of work they have been working on recently. The aim is to have something they can all do. *Have the full instruction written on the board (in the same place each time) before the pupils arrive.* Tell them as they reach the door individually or in groups.

On other occasions, however, the teacher will have devised a simple short 'limbering up' exercise. If you are in your early months of teaching or if the class is particularly difficult, go to the trouble of setting the slip of paper and/or worksheet out on each desk before the pupils arrive. Once again, your word at the door is reinforced by your written instructions on the board.

In each case, use the five minutes of silent work to sort out quietly any late-comers, those who have not brought the necessary pen or books, etc. (I should recommend that the work is normally carried out in complete silence and that you are strict about this.) Then, if the lesson is to involve exposition or question and answer, after the preliminary piece of work, call the pupils' attention and start your talk from the purposeful calm of that activity, whenever possible building on it and growing out of it. Often, of course, the initial activity will be to 'continue with last week's work'. In this case, the key is to get each pupil into it as soon as he enters. Again, don't wait until general talk has started. And you'll need to make sure that necessary equipment and books are out in advance.

Oversight

I have stressed throughout that as most misbehaviour is spont-aneous rather than long planned, it can be prevented merely by the 'withitness' of the teacher. Young teachers frequently concern themselves with what they should do when there is bad behaviour, not fully realizing that most examples of bad behav-iour would not happen if the pupils were under observation and knew it. Thus an important part of classroom technique is maintaining a constant surveillance of everything that is happening in the room. This means that the teacher's position in the room needs thought, and the posture in which he helps a pupil. For instance, it is almost impossible to keep an eye on the room whilst bending down from a standing position to help a seated pupil, but easy to keep an eye on the room whilst sitting at a desk with a pupil by your side. Obviously it is im-possible to see the room if a knot of pupils is between you and the others, or if you turn your back on the class. I have often been told quite clearly by pupils later found misbehaving that the act started when 'Sir was writing on the board with his back to us'.

A particular skill which needs practise is the ability to 'overlap' activities, so that the teacher can keep two activities going at once. Thus he must be able to deal with one pupil's minor mis-behaviour, or a late-comer's intrusion into the room, without breaking off completely from the ongoing activity, or without losing the oversight of the room. A classroom method that makes oversight impossible is simply an unsuitable method for school teaching. It is very rare for a pupil, for instance, to throw an exercise book out of a window when Sir is looking, but just the kind of thing that can happen when the teacher is deeply engrossed in helping another pupil.

The End of the Lesson

The end of a lesson is not merely the end of that lesson; it is part of the sequence that will lead to other lessons or activities in the school and will be remembered at the back of the pupils' minds as a cue for the tone of your next lesson. It should therefore be an orderly and pleasing occasion. Never let your relief at the end of a difficult lesson encourage you to sign off early, abruptly, or carelessly.

Consider, for instance, a teacher who had thirty second-year pupils working fairly well, if a little noisily. The bell went precisely on time by the classroom clock. A moment *afterwards* he said: 'Will you be packing up now. The bell's gone.' He *then* tried to gather up some of their books! Such an end was unfair on the pupils, and didn't help him. It was the end of the week; these pupils needed a summing up, a pat on the back, and re-assurance that he was pleased with the week and had a plan for the next. What's more, he ought to have got them out dead on time so that they could get to their next teacher on time.

The routine should have been something like this:

2.21 (and I mean as precisely as that) (*standing at the front of the room where they can all see, and stopping their work.*): Stop writing now. (*Insist on complete silence.*) I'm sorry to interrupt you when you're doing so well, but my next customers will be here soon. (*Or whatever joke you can manage.*) This week we've all written up our pieces for the exhibition, and I'm looking forward to reading them. Next week we're going to do a longer piece of writing. Collect up your pieces now.

2.22 Without talking, check your name is on each and hand your piece to John or Fred. Will you collect them up please. (*These pupils do, in the usual order.*)

2.23 Please put your books away in silence. Check there're no bits of paper on the floor. (*John and Fred bring the work to you.*)

2.24 Without scraping your chairs, please stand. (*You go over to the door.*)

2.25 (*Bell goes*): Well, that was a good week, I look forward to seeing you on Tuesday and I'll tell your Form Master how well you've done. This row out first, please. (*You stand in the open door, seeing them out, saying the odd word to individuals, and keeping an eye on the corridor.*)

It is normally wise to ask a class to leave the room a group or a row at a time. This is not always necessary with older pupils, larger rooms, or smaller classes. However, avoid a rush and dismiss a line at a time if you are in doubt. Stand in your earlier position against the door jamb. There you can again supervise room and corridor, and at the same time give each pupil a pleasant parting word or a reminder as appropriate.

Pupils' Written Work

Be warned, many of your pupils in the course of the year will lose much of their work, even when they have done well and are proud of it. It is worth thought and care to try to help them avoid this. Consider the various ways of storing work. A Junior-school pupil spends almost all his week in one room and keeps all his books in his own desk. He rarely takes them home, and therefore his only organizational problem is to keep that desk tidy enough for his books to be accessible. The Secondary pupil, who moves from teacher to teacher and takes books home for homework, has a more difficult organizational problem. How can the teacher help?

The safest way is to reduce the amount of written work, whether notes or projects, which the pupil has to keep himself. The most effective safeguard is to issue the pupil with a simple loose-leaf folder, which is to be used only for the temporary filing of work in progress. (In the case of very long projects, this must mean only for the section being currently worked on.) All written work is done on punched file-paper. The 'current' folder is thus *never* handed in, but each piece or section of work that the teacher wants to take away to read is handed in apart from the folder. *Completed* pieces of work, after teacher and pupil have reviewed them, are filed by the teacher in the pupil's personal 'deposit' file, which the teacher stores. From time to time these are issued for sorting, reviewing, and maybe index-ing sessions, and the folder can also be used for notes of indi-vidual teacher/pupil talks, other relevant non-confidential material, and so on. Even the scattiest pupil begins to be impressed by the growing body of his work, and the most he can lose at any one time is a single piece!

There are of course other patterns. The pupil can use his loose-leaf folder as his cumulative file, handing in only indi-vidual pieces as before. He again has only one, but always one, folder to remember. This is less trouble for the teacher, but risks a year's work being lost in one moment. Many schools prefer to use exercise books, which are definitely more econo-mical on paper as work can start immediately after the pre-ceeding piece of writing. If you use exercise books, have a clear routine for them. There is little more infuriating than the constant arguments about whether 'Sir' has the book or not, and if it has been lost, who lost it. The old convention of one book for 'classwork' and one for 'homework' is a possible method, but it does not seem very convenient to me. Better to have an 'A' and a 'B' book, specify which is to be used, make a note in your register, and always have one in and one out. I really find, however, that only the most reliable groups can properly manage this. My paper and two folders scheme works for classes with somewhat high absentee rates and low organizational ability, but could be challenged as not encouraging the pupil to organize and care for his own materials.

Collecting In and Giving Out Work

A potential trouble point, which disturbs the atmosphere and tempts pupils into misbehaviour, is the returning of work read by the teacher to the class. In some kinds of learning sequences, such as extended project work, the teacher is not faced with the simultaneous return of thirty pieces of paper, folders, or exercise books. However, it is a frequent situation in all kinds of subject and all kinds of pupil groupings to have to give out thirty pieces of paper, folders, or exercise books as economically as possible.

Like me, you probably have a fairly clear picture at the back of your mind of a schoolmaster of old talking to thirty boys whilst with calculated inaccuracy he flings books through the air into different directions. No one makes any noise. Every boy is attentive. The teacher's virtuoso display of eccentric markmanship is rapid, quells the class, and even allows a few teaching points to be made mid-stream. Those days have gone! I have seen more lessons founder as the ill-prepared teacher copes with this apparently simple chore than at almost any moment in the lesson. The teacher revolves hopelessly, trying to give or throw books in criss-crossing directions, not sure which book will come next, or where each pupil is. Those waiting have nothing to do. Those who have received their books give them a momentary glance and join in the fun. Then there is an exchange of disputes as some pupils say they haven't had their books. The teacher is uncertain who has not had a book, and if not, why not. The whole procedure is protracted by useless disputes.

I suggest a clear and regularly repeated routine. I shall describe it as if, as I have recommended, the pupils are seated in alphabetical order parallel with your class register. However, the basic procedures can stand with only a little obvious modification if the seating does not follow this pattern. The aims of the routine are two-fold: firstly, a clear and well-known routine stops arguments about who has and who has not handed in work; these are not merely unprofitable but sour relationships and tempt any would-be malingerers into exploiting the confusion to cover up their defaulting. Secondly, a clear-cut routine avoids the waiting and confusion in the room.

When you collect in the books, do so in a fixed and precisely repeated routine. Preferably follow the seating plan so that the books are in the order of your mark register. Have the books collected in whilst the pupils are engaged in some sensible activity – never make collecting in an unaccompanied activity during which pupils are expected to wait patiently. They won't. Whenever possible, collect them at a suitable point *during* the lesson – not in the last minutes. This allows the collecting to be done calmly and carefully. It also allows time for you to check up with any individuals who have not handed work in. If you don't wish to go round yourself collecting the books, arrange for *regular* pupils to do so. More than one, to save time; but not too many, to save movement. I like the first and last in the alphabetical sequence to work from either end. Double-check the books – that is, enter a mark in your register (see page 37) to indicate that you have received the book from a pupil, and count the pile of books and check that the number tallies with the number of heads in the room. Quite a proportion of pupils work on the principle that a confrontation postponed may be a confrontation avoided. They therefore do not declare a failure to produce work at this stage, and hope that it will be discovered too late. They will even hand in a book despite the fact that it has no work in it. Too frequently the teacher is sufficiently confused for it to be possible for such a sharp trickster to get away with it, and thus to be encouraged to try again. I therefore prefer the work to be left open on the pupil's desk before collection, and to collect it myself.

The returning of work is naturally the reverse process. Any mark or grade will have been entered into the mark register in advance. The pile is still in seating order. The class are told that the books will be given out shortly, and if there is anything specific that they should look for or do on receiving their books. At a time when they are engaged on some work, the books are brought round. This is a simple and unfussy job as the pile is in seating order and a slow walk round the room suffices. I prefer to do this myself on most occasions as I can add a quiet personal word to a number of pupils. Separate any teaching comments you might wish to make to the whole class from the actual distribution of the papers. This is partly because no one listens if his neighbour has just had a book back, and partly because it is very difficult to teach and hand back simultaneously. There is nothing more baffling than trying to listen to a teacher who is darting around the room with books. When you get to the distribution, a variation on this is to lay the books out on the appropriate desks before the pupils reach the room. This leads naturally to starting the lesson with the pupils picking up some point from their returned books. One teacher of Science had the excellent scheme of having the books in a manilla folder for each work-bench, which was labelled with a colour, and this colour was the same as that for the relevant folder.

Whatever your teaching style you will have to cope with this basic task of collecting and returning written work hundreds of times every week. It is therefore worth working out a routine which:

allows reliable record-keeping;
eliminates disputes;
is quiet and quick;
is simple and efficient;
never keeps the pupils waiting.

Materials and Equipment

Many lessons require the frequent use of various kinds of equipment which has to be issued for the particular lesson, one item to each pupil or group of pupils. The handling of these can be a nightmare for a young teacher, and any losses can cause inconvenience, loss of time, and irritation for subsequent lessons. As in every other matter, the starting point is preparation: check in advance that you have sufficient protractors, scissors, test tubes, or work-cards, that you know precisely how many there are, and that the supply is ready to hand. Ideally, the equipment is best stored in a sectional tray of some sort that shows at a glance how many items are there and if any are missing. Preferably, small items, such as scissors, should be stored in trays or racks that hold sufficient only for one-third or half of the class. This speeds up distribution and collection, and is far easier. An obvious example of such storage is pencils: kept and displayed in a block of wood with drilled holes, their checking is easy. Chime bars for music lessons are a different example of the same need. A compartmental shallow drawer for, say, eight, with a beater in each compartment, makes it possible to see at a glance that each chime bar and beater has been returned. Or you may prefer to store the beaters separately in racks similar to those for test tubes, so that you can see the precise number of beaters at the start and at the finish. The same principle also applies to the distribution of books or returnable work-cards. If they are pre-piled in, say, tens, there is a clear visual check. Work-cards are conveniently stored in stout envelopes which have been cut back at the top to reveal the front of the contents.

Whenever you are going to issue anything to the whole class, announce what is going to be issued and how: e.g. 'The girl at the front of each row will bring the tray down the row. Take one each.' Add clearly the number that there are to start with, and when they will be collected; e.g. 'There are ten in each tray, that's thirty altogether. I shall collect all thirty books into the trays a quarter of an hour before the end of the lesson.' It is then a good idea to write the number of items on the board in a prominent position (a regular position if yours is an equipment-orientated subject such as Music or Science):

Tuesday, 11 November
30 rulers.

If you have taken care over the preparation and issuing, collection and checking will be easy. Don't leave it to the last minute, but do make sure the pupils have something else to do whilst the collection is going on. Nothing is more boring than collection as a sole activity. Give due warning: 'We shall collect the rulers in five minutes.' Then announce the collection method clearly, preferably using the same pupils as those who did the distribution: 'Will the girls in the front of each row please take a tray each and collect a ruler back from everyone in that row. We started with thirty rulers, and I shall check that we have thirty back.' The front girls then do the collection whilst the pupils are doing some writing. Rapidly check the returned trays to make sure each is complete. If one tray has an item short, confidently go down that row at once, saying: 'There's one more to come from this row still.' When you have completed the checking, which should be very quick, let the class know that all is well: 'Good, we have every one of the thirty rulers back.' It is worth declaring this, both because you want the message to be taken clearly that you always check and always know, and also because it ends the lesson with a certain feeling of satisfaction. Pupils *like* being members of a well-run and well-behaved group. If you have not received all the items back, make an immediate and confident fuss. It is a difficult question of tact to decide how much fuss. You will see why initial checking is so important: you cannot in all conscience challenge a class to 'Return the missing lens' if you are not absolutely sure how many you started with. You will also see the value of the sectional storage and distribution: it narrows the missing item down to one sector of the class. If you are indeed confident that a lens, a magnet, a pair of scissors, a book, or a chime-bar beater is missing, my advice is to hold the class and send immediately for a senior colleague. If you do this on the first occasion when an item is missing, the problem will not recur. Teachers in Science, Music, Maths, and Crafts especially have to be willing to be very firm and to call for support to find the missing item *immediately*. To allow a group to get away with a stolen ruler is to collude with the theft. To regard some items as too small to worry about is to encourage larger thefts.

There is no doubt that the kind of procedures which I have described are economical of time in the long run, and apply equally to mixed-ability or setted work, to 'formal' or 'informal' methods, to 'discovery' or 'didactic' lessons. You must get the apparatus out quickly and you must get it all back efficiently.

Worksheets, etc.

In the previous section I have concentrated on the issuing of items of equipment or apparatus, and to some extent books or work-cards involve the same procedures. But in addition, there is for them the problem of explanation and of the pupil's need to read. These problems have nothing to do with security and apply equally to disposable sheets which you will not be collecting up. When issuing a worksheet, map, or diagram, remember that for most pupils it is difficult to listen carefully *and* scan a fresh page. Therefore divide the process into three:

a. Explain that a sheet is about to be given to each. It is about such-and-such; its purpose is so-and-so; and each pupil will be expected to do this or that. 'When you first get the sheets, put your name in the box, . . .' (It is vital that each pupil has a clear task for when the sheet is received.)

b. Have the sheets given out (see page 52) as rapidly as possible, and in silence – yours and theirs! (It is futile to call out instructions *over* a distribution process.)

c. After a moment for the task, call for attention. Explain the purpose of the sheet briefly a second time. Take the pupils through its sections. Give the instructions for action a second time. Ask for questions. Only then can the pupils start work on their own. Without this careful procedure there will be a scatter of questions, the answers to which will not be heard by the whole class as most will still be reading.

There will be many occasions when pupils are expected to draw a fresh assignment card, whether from an SRA 'Reading Laboratory' or a set of teacher-prepared sheets, at their own timing according to their completion of their last task. This is likely to be especially common in mixed-ability classes. In such cases, the various sheets or cards are likely to be part of a consistent series, and it is then worth a patient initial lesson making quite sure that the procedures and conventions of the cards are thoroughly understood.

Supplies

Many lessons are going to require pupils to have access throughout to fresh supplies, especially of paper, sometimes of assignment cards, books, or chemicals. Establish a clear and unvarying prominent position for the supply. If a great deal of paper is to be used, two piles on either side of the room, under your eye, should be put out regularly before each lesson. It is often worth fixing a route to avoid chair scraping and pushing. Make it clear whether permission has to be sought, or the pupil in need may merely leave his chair to fetch the material. If in the early days you make position, manner, and mode clear ('no dashing'!), in the future this servicing of the learning will normally go smoothly. Never have to delve into a stockroom mid-lesson. An almost invariable rule is to do without what you haven't brought.

Moving Furniture or Re-Grouping

One of the most rapid ways to produce chaos is to instruct a group as a whole to move themselves, or even worse themselves and some furniture, to a new, vaguely described position. 'Get your chairs round me' or some such general instruction is a formula for noisy lengthy muddle, with lost tempers and bruised shins. Yet it is fairly often necessary to arrange such re-groupings. Pupils may need to be re-seated in a closer group to watch a film-loop projected on a screen; they may need to break into small discussion groups; for a competition, they may need to face inwards in two teams; two classes may need to come together in one room to watch a film; in a drama class, a special seating arrangement may be necessary for some group activity. In all cases, it is the teacher's job to *organize* such a move to make it as economical of time, effort and temper as possible. Such a move will not be achieved successfully without careful and precise teacher direction, unless it is a frequent manoeuvre which works to a regular routine.

The art of directing a large group of pupils in any complicated manoeuvre is to break the group down so that reasonably small numbers carry out clearly understood actions in turn. This means that the teacher must first be clear exactly what is required. I have seen a whole class moving with chairs above their heads, knocking into each other and jockeying for positions in the new arrangement, with the teacher trying to shout over the top some new set of directions. Be clear where you want the pupils, and be sure they'll fit in the new positions.

Then call for complete silence and attention. Explain that you are about to give some directions for movement, but that *no one is to move until they are actually told to*. This last is a vital convention to establish and needs building habitually into every set of movement instructions. Otherwise, with the very best of intentions, pupils start moving and following the teacher's instructions in mid-sentence. Others then follow them; the teacher stops the instruction to tell them to wait; the first lot move back and knock into the next wave. Minor chaos again reigns. Therefore get used to warning 'No movement until I say so' *before* you start delivering the instructions.

Then state specifically which pupils, in which order, are to move to which position. Normally it is best to give the instructions in sections, having each sub-group of pupils move at the appropriate moment. Thus the problem may be to re-group the pupils *and their chairs* in a tight semi-circle of two rows in a part of the room where there is space so that, shall we say, they can provide a concentrated audience for three pupils who have prepared a small dramatic reading or performance. The best way to do this would be to tell the pupils earlier that, before they have finished their writing, you will be telling them how to move to their special seating. At the appropriate moment tell the four performers to stay in their seats. Say: 'The row by the door *only*, when I say so, lift your chairs quietly, walk down the aisle and, in the same order, put your chairs down facing the performers' table. Right, *move*, please.' After that group has settled, a similar instruction brings the middle row. Then the first half of the window row joins the semi-circle. And finally the last five in the middle row move to sit on the window benches. It is thus possible to re-seat the class quickly and quietly, by dividing the larger group into sections and giving instructions and initiating movement for only one section at a time.

Modern mixed-ability teaching frequently uses group-work. There are therefore going to be times when the teacher requires the class to change into group positions. It is my firm practice to note the groupings in my mark book by a designated letter against each pupil's name. I then call out the names of 'Group A', and ask them to move. And then 'Group B'. I thus avoid criss-crossing movements and traffic jams with the legs of upraised chairs clashing and locking. Such movements are also frequent in science.

There is a similar problem if the class is to be taken mid-lesson from their normal room to another classroom, or for a Fire Drill. If the teacher goes first, he cannot lock the door behind him and he cannot be sure that two or three don't linger. If he follows last, he cannot be sure what is happening at the front, nor what will happen when the first reach the new venue. Either way, the line will straggle. There is a necessary two-stage procedure which works: the teacher goes to the door as for normal dismissal from the rooms. Before instructing the class to lead on, he tells them to line up in the corridor just outside his room. He then supervises the exit, locks the door, goes to the *front* of the line, and only then starts the second stage of leading the pupils on. This two-stage procedure makes the whole exercise much easier and more pleasant.

The general rule is simple: don't involve your pupils in movement unless it is really valuable. If you really want the movement, give precise instructions for sub-groups of pupils only at one time. To be able to move a group of, say, thirty pupils is a necessary skill for a teacher.

Curtains, Blinds, and Screens

One wishes one could do without them, but most of us teach in rooms with the three hazards of cords, blinds (or curtains), and screens. Indeed, teachers without blackout or screens frequently ask for them to be fitted. But they can be the source of a great deal of trouble – as can ordinary windows. Closing the curtains, raising a blind, or lowering a roller screen are all tricky operations. If the operator pulls too hard or lets go too quickly, damage can result which will not only be a nuisance but will probably leave the offending object in such a way that another person will seize it later and damage it still further.

At the start of a lesson, as the third-years come noisily in, the first bunch sees a projector.

'Is it films today, sir?' one asks.

The teacher should have set the projector up in advance, but he's still untangling the speaker lead, and is slightly nervous about lacing the film. 'Yes,' he shouts, 'And settle down quickly'. This, of course, is never likely to happen after such a vaguely phrased exhortation delivered in the direction of the back wall as he hurries to the mains socket.

'Do you want the curtains shut?' a helpful lad yells out.

'Of course, dope!' a girl calls back. 'Do you think we're going to see a film in this sunshine?'

'I'll do them,' another boy offers.

The teacher is too busy with the sprockets to do more than yell, 'Yes, but be careful'.

His wishful thinking is disappointed as two boys go for one curtain. Another unravels the screen cord, and it comes down with a heavy thump, which tells the informed ear that it will never rise again. Another curtain has apparently stuck, and a yank in the reverse direction from a boy, who (like boys usually do) is hanging on as low down the curtain as possible, tears the rufflette tape off for two feet or so.

After the film, the screen hangs forlornly, one curtain won't return, another has a gash where it caught the corner of an open window, and a third limps from the torn rufflette. These, of course, then require extra care, but actually get even rougher, despairing treatment. And all this from well-meaning, well-motivated, helpful pupils.

The safest way is to determine in advance that only the teacher will touch whichever of these three hazards your room boasts. Announce this clearly and stick to it. If you feel this is too restrictive a way, and you will need the curtains closed too often for this, insist that only those pupils whom you instruct are ever to touch these items. You can then give specific instruction to certain pupils to carry out certain tasks. You can appoint one boy to the screen and one to each pair of curtains. They can have a little tuition in the quirks and delicacies of each. They'll think 'Sir is a bit fussy', but they'll be proud of their task and their expertise – and your curtains, blinds and screen will continue to serve you.

Leaving the Room

Well-meaning, sympathetic teachers are often perplexed by the requests they receive from pupils who ask to leave the room for a variety of personal or apparently educational reasons. The curt advice of those who say 'Never believe a word' seems harsh and hardly helpful to an understanding relationship, and yet the suspicion nags at the back of the mind that there *is* an unusually large number of requests and some pupils do seem to be thoughtlessly flitting in and out. Then comes some crisis, perhaps an accusation of vandalism or petty pilfering, and the teacher feels guilty at not having a tighter regime. There is also a real, though often unconscious, temptation for teachers, having control difficulties to allow a very high number of pupils out of the room to go to the library, the lavatory, to pick up forgotten books, or to check up on this that or the other. I found some American High Schools countering what they dubbed this 'clean-house policy' by issuing each teacher with one wooden tally. Only the tally was accepted as identification by the corridor security patrols, and thus the teacher could let only one pupil out at a time. Such a system is alien to our schools but it is a reminder that the problem is world-wide.

A teacher's classroom responsibility is to help his pupils learn. This normally involves keeping them in the learning room. Any learning reasons for sending a pupil out should be carefully pondered, authorized by the school's system, and identified by a dated note from the teacher. Personal reasons, such as visiting the lavatory or collecting a book, should be filtered down to an absolute minimum. It is perfectly possible for almost all pupils on almost all occasions to be ready for a lesson and not to require to go out again. If the teacher makes this clear, the need arises less. Remember also, any pupil who is giving you trouble in a class is likely to give trouble to the librarian, and to cause trouble in corridors, on staircases, and in lavatories. Further, his return is likely to be another of those disruptive moments.

Never send messages to another teacher's room for additional supplies of books or equipment. This disrupts two lessons and is indefensible. The longer I teach the more I dislike any interruption in my classroom. The atmosphere is very easily broken. If you think this odd, remember any occasions when a college or public reference library has been similarly disturbed: a ripple of dissatisfaction runs round all the readers who a moment ago had been deep in their books. Keep your own pupils.

Getting the Teacher's Attention

The accepted convention, which pupils take to readily, is for the pupil who needs the teacher's attention to raise his or her hand. If this convention is to work pleasantly and efficiently for teacher and taught, there are three simple and obvious common-sense rules: (a) The teacher must be able to *see* the raised hands! This means he must be in a position to see. (b) The pupils must be discouraged from asking too often or too readily. Don't misunderstand this remark, or interpret it as being callous. A little simple arithmetic shows that however hard you work, too many raised hands means no one gets a satisfactory reply. (c) The raised hand should *never* be accompanied by a call. If you allow 'Sir, sir, sir!', no one will be able to concentrate. These simple procedures are a sensible form of courtesy to the children as well as helping to keep the teacher's sanity. They are basically those operated in adult committees and meetings, and this is a point worth making to the class.

The Question of Noise

One of the greatest problems is the almost theological one of defining 'reasonable noise'. Frequently, a teacher feels that some talking is not only reasonable but desirable, but finds the level rises until he or she can not be heard and very few people can work. I should suggest that pure silence is often easier, fairer, and more pleasant. It also releases the teacher to help individuals instead of acting as a continuous noise queller. The teacher must therefore decide when talking is really useful to the activity, as for instance in group experiments in Science. Criteria for what talking is acceptable and what is not should be defined in advance. Too often one hears vague, broadside criticisms thrown at a class in an attempt to control what has become by even the most accepting standards unacceptable noise:

'That's quite enough noise, 2L.'

'You're getting too noisy again, you know.'

These remarks, which have to be shouted above the on-going noise and thus add to it, are too vague to give any pupil a clear instruction. Perhaps the worst I have heard was the desperate shout:

'Will you make less noise and do more work!'

These pleas have insufficient clarity. The general hubbub is marginally reduced for a short time, and then it builds up to the same or an even worse level.

If talking is to be allowed, the criteria can usually be defined more precisely and helpfully by legislating about to whom the talking may be directed:

'You may talk to your partner, but *not* across the gangways or to anybody in a different row.'

'Members may talk to anyone within their group, but you must not talk to anyone in another group.'

'Only one person at a time may talk, and the group leader, who is chairman, will decide who is to talk next.'

It is more difficult to define acceptable voice levels, as the distinction between 'talking' and 'shouting' is vague, and hardly sensed by many young people. Nevertheless, instead of directing criticisms to the class as a whole about the level of noise as a whole, it is possible to patiently pick on each of the loud pupils one by one (for there is usually a handful who are considerably louder than the others), speak to them individually, and by a mixture of joking and firmness to train them to speak 'quietly'. If you do not, they will be the ones who ignore your general pleas to the whole class, and they will act as pacers, encouraging the whole class gradually to get louder and more disruptive week by week.

There is an easy assumption that for some reason or other talking is a necessary part of all mixed-ability work. Certainly, talking for a purpose is an essential part of much learning. Recent research has usefully emphasized that for us. However, that does not mean that it is valuable *all* the time. Much individual work, especially reading and writing, requires an atmosphere of concentration. For these activities the silence of a public library is normally far more succesful than 'reasonable noise', and is much appreciated by most pupils. Indeed it is more enjoyable to have clearly defined contrasts between the 'co-operative talking' and the 'library silence' sessions than it is to have all lessons at roughly similar level of interruptive noise, with the teacher struggling to regulate the volume every fifteen minutes or so.

Helping the Individual

One of the greatest technical problems, and one which ruins many good intentions, is how to give individual help to pupils. It is a necessary part of mixed-ability work, or Nuffield Science, or many Humanities schemes. Yet so often all that happens is that no one gets any real attention and the general class atmosphere makes it difficult for anyone to work. *Effective personal help requires ruthless method.* If you are to have a proper consultation with a single pupil, you must be reasonably sure you will not be interrupted by other pupils. There is little more depressing for a pupil than the kind of lesson where the teacher is starting a few words to one pupil, breaks off to shout across the room, moves to another pupil, starts working with him, and turns in mid-sentence to quell trouble in another corner. I have seen this happen in lesson after lesson.

I remember one well-meaning and intelligent teacher with considerable presence, who easily reduced a class to a frustrated muddle. She was constantly and exhaustingly on the move and could never oversee the room. Concentration was made more difficult by 'Miss, miss, miss!' continuously from all over the room. The situation reminded me of a hotel waiter I was told of years ago in a large hotel lounge at tea time. He eventually became so irritated by the finger snapping and whistles that he flipped up the tails of his tailcoat, declaring: 'I may have a tail, but I am not a dog!' A teacher, similarly, is not a dog to be called like that. A teacher who finds this happening should ask himself why the pupils call. It is usually, firstly, that if one is allowed to, the others feel they must. Secondly, if the teacher constantly roves, he usually has his back to many of the pupils at any one time, thus forcing them to add voices to hands to catch attention. The teacher is exhausted and confused by the constant swivelling around, as he is tugged hither and thither.

The number of pupils you can see in a double lesson is limited if you are really going to help them. It is therefore better to reduce the number, but give effective help, and to keep a record so that you know clearly who has been seen and who missed. This may mean staying at your desk in the front of the room to do your individual helping. You are comfortable and stable, and able to talk more coherently. You can more easily keep the others quiet by a look without interrupting your work with the pupil. You have your mark register at hand to enter comments. The pupils know where you are. I myself have a chair by my right, and call pupils up with their work and Diary to sit by me for a few minutes at a time. Obviously, in a practical lesson, such as Science, you must move to the apparatus. It is then necessary for a very strict agreement that no one calls out. It is usually best to move in a regular circuit of the pairs or groups so that, even though you are on the move, the class have a sense of your direction.

Whatever you do, don't bury yourself in a knot of pupils, thus encouraging the others to cause a disturbance.

Group Work

All that I have said applies equally to working in groups and to working as a class or individually. However, group work brings with it advantages and difficulties in management. For instance, the advantage of giving pupils opportunities to co-operate can be lost if either rows or jokes become common. As the teacher is less often in a dominant position, it is often hoped that teacher-pupil relationships will be better. Too often, however, there is a bad effect on the teacher-pupil relationship, as the teacher turns into a wandering nagger, constantly harrying groups along, rarely able to teach, and thus losing his satisfaction as the pupils lose their contact with him. Group work has long been common in Drama, English, and especially Science, where both practical considerations of availability of equipment and educational ones requiring shared discussion towards deduction have made it essential.

It is now becoming more popular with teachers in the Humanities, Mathematics, Music, and even Languages. Many see it as the solution to the problems of mixed-ability teaching. Do not be tempted by group work merely as a current vogue, and do not see it as a panacea for mixed-ability problems.

Decide whether group work is likely to help in your particular situation by assessing the needs of the class and the advantages of working in groups. Groups offer the need to co-operate. They are therefore a better situation for planning, deducing, or analysing. Further, a small group offers the opportunity for pupils with more precisely defined qualities to interact (e.g. friends, withdrawn pupils, verbally able pupils, mechanically minded ones, a mixture of abilities). It is unlikely, even in Science or Drama, that all the work benefits very much from these characteristics, and the first essential of your planning is to *decide when and for what activities work in small groups is really best* (not, usually, for reading or writing). My advice is not to break a new class into groups too early – not until you have had a successful run of class and individual work.

Your decision about which activity to concentrate on will determine the composition of the group. There is a great deal of confused thinking about the use of small groups in mixed-ability classes, especially about whether the aim is to reproduce the mixture in the smaller group or give the opportunity of specially focused appropriate help to groups with roughly the same needs. It is odd that many inexperienced teachers automatically presume that 'group work' means work in self-chosen groups. There are three main grouping strategies:

1. ENTIRELY MIXED-ABILITY. Especially good for the verbal interaction of the less able pupils in activities that don't depend too much on intellect – e.g. planning a play in Drama, observing an experiment in Science, devising a sound pattern in Music, or interviewing a visitor in Social Studies.

2. CHOSEN FOR A SPECIFIC QUALITY. This may be necessary for emotional reasons or intellectual ones. For instance, it is often extremely difficult for shy and withdrawn pupils to join in group work in Drama in a group that has talented extroverts. A specially chosen 'shy' group can work better on occasions. Similarly, in some scientific work pupils who have difficulties with computation may be better working together, so that they can be given special help and will participate. When group

work is used in languages, pupils are usually best with others of their own language ability. The decision is influenced by the nature of the activity: will pupils gain or have extra difficulties if the small groups have a mixture of a certain kind of ability?

3. FRIENDSHIP GROUPS. Obviously self-chosen groups will not necessarily be formed according to either 1 or 2. For certain activities, old friendships will help by offering security and support. *For others, precisely the opposite effect will result.* The arguments I gave earlier about pupil seating (page 27) apply even more forcefully here.

Having decided when to break into groups and which kind of group, tell the pupils of the plan and the grouping method. If you simply slip into your explanation of the Art project or the Mathematics scheme '... and we shall work in groups', there will be a tic-tac display of signalling across the room for surreptitious recruiting, which will completely blot out your explanation from the pupils' minds. Make it clear how the groups will be arranged:

'I have already divided you up into five groups.'

'Your group letter is on the top of the work I handed back.'

'You can choose your own groups during break, and write down the names of those you wish to work with before we meet again.'

I personally plan groups in my mark book, sometimes having lettered heterogeneous groups and numbered homogeneous ones, calling on them as appropriate. I very rarely allow self-chosen friendship groups for I have found in subjects as diverse as Mathematics and Drama that the results are less good.

What size should the groups be? This depends on the characteristics of the activity, the room, and the pupils. For most rooms, six groups is the maximum that can work separately without mutual distraction. Five is a better number in a normal-sized room – one in each corner and one in the centre. Science labs are usually larger and can take more groups. Subjects that work in smaller class sizes can similarly have smaller groups. As for the size of the group, five seems the ideal number for most activities. If the group is above six, a leader is required and problems of control start up. If the group is below four, interaction can become less profitable.

The teacher must brief the class very closely about the task of each group. Usually the tasks should be precisely defined, often involving reporting back. Whilst the groups are operating, the teacher's role is difficult. Above all, he must retain overall control. Far from group work being the key to class control, as some teachers optimistically hope, *class control is the key to group work*. For part of the time you may have to stand in your central focal point merely giving out a benign but firm look and nudging one or two pupils into their group activity by a look. Later you may wish to walk around *without intervening* but simply looking encouragingly at each group close to. These two tasks are necessary, for the work of the group is likely still to depend on your observable interest, seen from afar.

The most difficult task is to give more precise encouragment to each group. It is a great skill to be able to visit each group quickly and effectively, and one which is acquired only by conscious practice. You will not be able to go far with any one group. Therefore, be clear what enquiry you are going to make to each group, and avoid a cosy little chat. Make your enquiry precise:

'What colours have you seen in the test tubes?'
rather than:
'And how's it all going?'
'What scale have you chosen for the plan?'
rather than:
'And is the plan working out?'

Normally you will have to settle for one or two such enquiries, a comment on the answer, or a phrase of encouragement, and you will move on. Move irregularly but calmly, so that your circuit is not regular enough for skivers to know when you'll reach them. If another group does make a distracting noise whilst you are working with one group, finish what you are doing and then move across. If points of general value strike you as you observe the work of various groups, save the points up. You can then stop *all* the work and make one group of points to the whole class from a good focal point. Don't throw out snippets of advice to the whole class unexpectedly from different corners of the room.

If you are going to use group work, be judicious in choosing your opportunity, thoughtful in the composition of the groups, specific in your instructions, and firm in your overall control.

6 The Teacher's Performance

Of all the unfashionable points which I need to make, my central idea here may well be the most unacceptable. My experience and observation convince me that, whether he likes it or not, every Secondary-school teacher is to some extent a performer. A teacher of a group of pupils is often projecting himself to the group. He will neither convey the sense of an explanation nor the feeling of his reaction unless he has developed ways of amplifying and projecting to the group.

Every teacher has to cultivate a certain air of confidence. This is not the same as being over-bearing, or brash, or domineering. There is, though, in any audience (and a teacher forgets at his peril that, however he is teaching, the pupils are often an audience) a subtle sixth sense that alerts them to a lack of confidence in the person 'out there'. In pupils, as in music-hall audiences of the past, there is further an instinct that drives them to test that hint of a lack of confidence, and to split the person apart if it proves as weak as it appears. This is neither to recommend insincerity nor to demand constant volume. A teacher needs to be true to himself, and his 'performing' ability is part of that. To be 'larger than life' is not to be false to life, but it is to select and develop. In this section I shall consider various aspects of this 'performing'.

Appearance

The days when Headteachers insisted on dark suits for teachers have long gone. Indeed, so have the days, in most Secondary schools, when a Headteacher even feels able to venture an opinion on teachers' dress, still less to proffer advice. Yet, there is no doubt that clothing speaks: the teacher's clothes and appearance are an important part of his classroom success. I have argued continually that the school in general and the classroom in particular are not just any old places, and that they have their necessary conventions. A teacher's clothing is part of that, and the pupils have certain expectations.

The first of these is an only half-conscious feeling that 'if he cares about us, he'll care about how he looks for us'. It is a normal expectation that respect and care for a situation will be reflected in care over the individual's appearance, and that this care, whatever its stylistic manifestation, will be revealed in cleanliness, good condition, and obvious signs of considered choice. Children from 'working-class' backgrounds especially expect teachers to be 'respectably' dressed. It is worth remembering, and pondering the implications, that the man in a pub on a Sunday in a well-off suburb will very likely be casually dressed in a sweater but his counterpart in a working-class area puts on his best clothes for the occasion. Similarly, working-class parents, recent immigrants, indeed most parents, dress carefully and somewhat formally for visits to school. It is an insensitive fallacy to think that these parents are made to feel more at their ease by a teacher dressed casually. Similarly, it is an odd and inaccurate interpretation of social class to presume, for instance, that children from deprived inner-city areas prefer their teachers to be either scruffy or *avant-garde*.

Most pupils' preferences are fairly clear: they like their teachers to be individually dressed, interestingly but not too unusually, colourfully but not too strikingly, neatly but not too staidly. Younger pupils will be heard to describe some women teachers approvingly as being dressed 'prettily'. They are thrown by the slightly aggressive uncertain choice of whatever is currently the way-out vogue; they are depressed by the badly worn; and they are insulted by the torn or dirty.

Speaking to the Class

There are going to be many times when you need to speak to the whole class. These must be a success, both because pupils enjoy being members of a class and these 'whole-class' moments are therefore important to them, and because if you cannot succeed on these occasions, that elusive control of the group will slip away from you. There are three clues to speaking to the whole class:

1. choose your moment;
2. decide what you're going to say;
3. use a suitable manner.

1. CHOOSE YOUR MOMENT. If everyone needs to hear, you

must make sure everyone does. Conversely, if everyone does not need to hear it, don't trouble to say it! A suitable moment must relate both to the function of what is being said and to the mood of the group. For instance, it is a bad moment while a few are not yet in the room, or while the class are putting materials away. You can see many teachers suddenly thinking of something that they think the class ought to know. All the pupils are busying around; the teacher suddenly starts throwing out a scatter of advice. No one is ready for it; many don't stop to listen; most others don't hear. Never pepper a buzz of activity with general instructions at odd moments. Such ill-judged outbursts do more harm than good. *Whenever you talk to the class, obtain complete silence.*

Be sure you need to talk. Gather in your mind all that you need to say. ('And one last thing . . .' is often used to introduce three or four points!) Then position yourself sensibly. (Never throw out advice on the move or from a back corner of the room.) Catch attention and silence – completely. A clap or a simple phrase can work.

'Right, stop work and listen, please.'
'Everyone quiet now!'
'Three B!'

Never start until you have both complete silence and all eyes on you. Remember, you have disciplined yourself not to speak unless it is necessary, and you have not got immediate silence and attention: keep calm and good-humoured. Hold your position and pause a moment. In a quieter and friendly tone speak to two or three pupils *by name*:

'John, you've got to put that down now.'
'Wendy, look at me.'
'Gay, stop talking now.'
(The importance of knowing the individual names is obvious.)

One, final, gathering exhortation is probably necessary now:

'Good. Everyone listen carefully!' or
'Right, everyone's looking at me, then!'

In some especially noisy situations such as improvised Drama, P.E., or 'workshop' Music sessions, it is often best to use a manufactured sound to call the class to silence. For instance, I've seen a tabor successfully used, and I myself use a cymbal in Music.

2. WHAT ARE YOU GOING TO SAY?   The old preacher's rule applies to almost all classroom speech:

Tell them what you're going to tell them.

Tell them.

Tell them what you've told them.

This is not boring: it makes for clarity and, most significantly, gives *confidence* to the listener, who can know where the speaker is going and know that he has grasped what he is meant to grasp. It is always easier to understand the detail of what is being said if the larger direction is clear and can be grasped.

Be concrete and particular. This may mean working up to a generalization by way of specific instances. It may mean avoiding the generalization altogether.

Use references and comparisons that the pupils are sure to have seen for themselves (or on the television screen) and have already recognized. It is amazing how often we use totally unknown comparisons – rural imagery to urban children.

Get into the way of putting sentences so that the central ideas come out clearly. This means that the key facts should not be subordinated, nor should they linger to the end of a sentence. Grammatically simple sentences are usually better than more sophisticated compound ones. 'Even though. . . .', 'It was because. . . .', 'Until they had completed. . . .', 'The fact that. . . .' are all examples of cliff-hanger openings that push the main point to the end of the sentence and frequently confuse. Avoid, then, long compound sentences with strings of parentheses and subordinate clauses. Such a sentence depends on the listener holding sections in his mind until the speaker returns to the main structure. Many pupils will have lost the thread by then.

There is also the problem of vocabulary (or, for pupils, 'Vocabulary is also a problem'). On the whole, this is less serious than syntax, but nevertheless care is needed. Any key technical words should, whenever possible, be written on the board in advance. Then they can be pointed to as you use them, and the sight reinforces the sound. Usually, you will want to avoid the less common words. Notice I do not say 'long' or even 'difficult'. The real test is which words have become familiar from the television and popular papers. Rather than avoid every uncommon or difficult word, slip in an alternative or brief explanation without holding up the flow of the sentence.

3. THE MANNER.   Talking to a class-size group is an art, and one that needs practising. It is neither the same as lecturing to

one hundred nor as chatting to two or three pupils in the park. It requires a mixture of both techniques. You need to have the right volume, a suitable range of expression, and the right communication of looks and eyes.

Your voice must be clear, and you must have a sense of speaking to the group. This is a skill that can be learnt. It means pitching your voice adequately for someone at the back, and maintaining that volume. Leave decent pauses between sentences and don't weaken your remarks with fill-in phrases such as 'kind of', 'sort of', 'y'know'. Although the volume must be adequate, the key is intensity and clarity rather than volume.

Pitch your voice a trifle higher than the level strictly required for full audibility, but only a trifle higher. Constant shouting is wearing to teacher and taught. On the other hand, a little spare volume, as it were, is necessary to prevent odd snatches being lost to some pupils. (Although you will sometimes wish to use a deliberately low volume for effect.) If you are faced with a specially large meeting, such as when three or more classes are brought together, perhaps as part of a team-teaching exercise, check first that you can be heard at the extreme back corners. Don't do this by a generalized 'Can you hear me at the back?'. This starts an embarrassed or raucous barrage. Instead ask one person specifically: 'John (or 'The boy by the door') please raise your hand if you can hear me satisfactorily.'

Modulate pitch, volume, pace, and tone both to suit the sense of what you are saying and for the almost musical effects that good speaking always has. Your face should, within sensible limits, reflect your voice. Your expression should change, your eyebrows rise, your mouth snap as the sense demands. It is curiously difficult to follow a deadpan face, as the incongruity between sense and look puzzles the hearer. Similarly, you should gesture economically but significantly.

Finally, the sense of speaking to the actual pupils present rather than merely delivering into the atmosphere comes from the way you manage to look at individuals and scan the group.

The key is the communication with your eyes. *Feel* the sectors of the room, and underline the structure and sequence of your remarks by directing your phrases to the different sectors. After a while you will come to do this naturally, using the change of direction as a form of rhetorical punctuation, not too abrupt or dramatic, but sufficient to help those in the room feel that they are a group, and that the words are embracing the entire room. Don't follow a regular circuit, like a radar beam remorselessly scanning the horizon. Think, perhaps, of the arrangement of a five on a dice: ∵ Take each of the five sectors into your glance from time to time in an irregular order. Within each group, look at only one pupil, a different one each time you return to the sector, and cast your remark to him. Feel that you really are communicating personally with that individual: look him or her in the eyes, and be aware of his or her expression. Almost never change direction arbitrarily mid-idea, but articulate the progress of the remarks and the shift of argument by the direction of focus. This way you establish an intimacy with the pupils that always assists order and enriches communication.

Questioning

It is taken for granted that teachers will ask questions, but an analysis of the purpose and method has not been properly attempted.[1] The paradox is that questions are, or should be, rarely asked for mere finding out, but more for teaching. That is, in asking the question the teacher is helping the pupil to focus and clarify, and thus to have thoughts and perceptions that he would not have had otherwise. When to ask a question, when not to, whom to ask it to, what to ask, how to point the question, how to know if a question is not registering – these are difficult skills. The point of the question is to teach rather than test. The question should therefore be answerable if at all possible. The skill is then the opposite of the questioning skill in a quiz or panel game, where the zest of battle drives towards 'winning'. The successful teacher's question is precisely one that *can* be answered, not one that can't be. Each question should be easy and short, building up a kind of programmed-learning approach to deeper or more difficult points. That way no one feels frustrated by facing the unanswerable, and the pupil is often able to see complex points as the culmination of 'obvious' simple points. This is, of course, as important in helping individuals as it is in full-class questioning, and is a key technique in Science and Mathematics.

Questions should not normally have a huge range of possible answers, except when you are building up a composite answer. These questions, which one hears so often in the classroom, are what I categorize as the 'Guess what I'm thinking' ques-

[1] See Barnes and Britton in the reading list on page 101 for a most valuable exploration.

tion: only telepathy can lead to the answer which the teacher has decided is 'the right answer'. Questions should be as specific as possible, and should be as pointed to the precise sequence of learning as possible.

Thus: 'What does a fraction mean?'

is not as good as: 'What does the figure beneath the line in a fraction tell you?'

Unless you are certain that the pupils fully understand all the terms of a question, avoid asking what is in effect two questions, in one.

Thus: 'What do the pyramids tell us about the Egyptians?'

Should be broken down into: 'What did the Egyptians use the pyramids for?' 'Why did they spend so much money and skill on that?'

Gap-filling is, on the whole, an unsatisfactory questioning technique; it encourages mere guessing and does not offer the benefit of a real exchange of thought. The typical kind of statement which ends with a sudden gap and a rising tone of voice to indicate the question also offers the very real difficulty that the pupil does not know a question is coming until it has gone! He then has to mentally replay the tape, as it were, to get back to the start of the sentence before he can answer it. No wonder classes bleat utter nonsense words in response to such questions.

Think twice before asking for the definition of a word. Abstract words are taxingly difficult to define, even by those who have a very good grasp of their meaning. A definition, furthermore, has to have a universal validity, whereas for the purposes of the learning of the moment only the relevant sense is required, thus the pupils groping for a full definition are often getting further from the problem rather than solving it. Examples of important words of which this is true are 'energy' in Science, 'relationship' in Mathematics, 'revolution' in History, or 'develop' in Social Studies. If you are requiring a definition, you must take trouble to get one. Pupils will more often than not give an instance ('It's when. . . .', 'A person who. . . .'). Thus, asked 'What does "impassive" mean?', pupils answer: 'When a person doesn't show his feelings.' So, if definition is not what you are working at, cast the question in a form that allows an example: 'If his face was "impassive" what would it show?'

The teacher has an important and sensitive task in responding to the pupil's answers also. A famous theatre producer, Tyrone Guthrie, once described the producer's central job as being 'an ideal audience of one'.[1] *The response is a form of teaching.* If you sit amongst the pupils in many lessons, you will be amazed at the number of answers that get no response at all, or merely a killing dead-flat 'yes'. Always give a clear, colourful, tactful response.

Despite your care, 'wrong' answers will frequently be given. Never mind. Use them for what they are – next steps to further thought – and take up the answer as a challenge for you to devise rapidly the next appropriate question. Never, or almost never, ridicule, but turn the answer to good account. It will be a guide to the pupil's misunderstanding. Don't labour the point. Explain a confusion. If there has been a misunderstanding, ask the question which clears it:

'If x is 3, what is $x - 2x$?'
'Minus two.'
(Clearly, the pupil answering has taken $x + 2$ away from x.)
'Oh? is 2x two *times* x, or two *plus* x?'
'Two times.'
'Then if x is 3, what does 2x equal?'
'Six.'
'Yes, because 2x is two *times* x, and two times 3 is six.'

The idea of clues needs care. If you are to prompt, do so by taking the pupil through the normal thought processes that would lead to the correct answer. Never merely give irrelevant verbal clues. Rhyme and association are not helpful to thought.

A central teaching technique which is of great pleasure to the pupils and of great value to their learning is a quick-fire sequence of questions ranging around the whole group, bringing all in, prompting thought and leading to understanding. As a general rule, always put the question before naming the pupil – otherwise no one else will think. Never start 'Does anyone know . . . ?' Vary the form and pattern of your questions, both to maintain interest and to make it impossible to guess who will be asked next. This can be an enjoyable game. Frequently require all the class to jot down short answers of one word or so on paper, and then ask one and then another to call an answer out. This not only makes it all like a party game, but also lets everyone participate. Sometimes use a show of hands as a way of making the class vote for one or another answer.

[1] A talk given before the Royal Society of Arts, 10 March 1952, and reprinted in *Directing the Play* by Toby Cole and Helen Krich Chinoy, Bobbs-Merrill Company, N.Y. 1962.

Reading Aloud

Most teachers have to read aloud at some point in their lessons. This is more so in the case of English teachers and slightly less so for other Humanities teachers. Even teachers of Mathematics or Science read aloud a surprising amount – far more than they seem to realize.

Reading aloud is not, in fact, a difficult skill, but it is one which is so rarely taught or practised in training that many teachers are extremely bad at it. There are few things more depressing than trying to concentrate on a teacher's dreary reading: voice flat, stumbling, failures of emphasis, speed a constant plod, eyes glued to the page, no gesture or movement, except for off-putting, irrelevant pacing around. No wonder a pupil once complained: 'When he reads, he makes it, well. . . . just a stream of words, not any sense.'

Bring out the speaking voice that lies behind the print. This means capturing the rhythmic pattern and bringing out the pauses. It means allowing the elision of those syllables that are elided in speaking. Keep the normal spoken pronunciation of 'a', 'say', 'had', rather than pedantically filling them out.

Practise on stories, where there is a real stimulus to animate the words on the page, to stress the dialogue, differentiate the speakers, dramatize the pauses, and read feelingly. Try, for instance, two stories by Bill Naughton,[1] manipulating the copy with one hand and holding the attention of the audience with your eyes. Can you realize the full comedy of *Seventeen Oranges*, when the lad Clem is preparing to steal a cheese from the docks and makes a dummy exit first?

> 'What have you got in there?' asked Pongo, who was the bobby on duty.
> 'A cat,' said Clem, 'but don't ask me to open it, or the blighter will get away.'
> 'A cat?' said Pongo. 'Don't come it. Let's have it opened.'
>   Clem wouldn't at first, but when Pongo insisted he got mad, and he flung it open, and out leapt a ship's cat, which darted back along the docks with Clem after it, shouting.'

The pause of expectation after 'he flung it open' is a fair test, as is the ending to a later story in the volume, one which moves the most 'difficult' and recalcitrant classes, *Spit Nolan*:

[1] *The Goalkeeper's Revenge and Other Stories*, Heinemann, New Windmill Series, 1967.

Then I heard the ambulance men asking me Spit's name.
Then he touched me on the elbow with his pencil and said:
'Where *did* he live?'
I knew then. The word 'did' struck right into me. But for
a minute I couldn't answer. I had to think hard, for the way
he said it made it suddenly seem as though Spit Nolan had
been dead and gone for ages.

Progress to practise illustrative material from history, and
descriptions in scientific writing. Include practice in articulat-
ing the explanations and questions in a Maths textbook. In
every case, practise actually standing, reading at full volume,
with your copy in your hands, and your eyes taking up members of the imaginary class. By the way, use the left hand to
cradle the book and the right hand to keep your place. That way
you can really dare to look up and know that you can return
to find your place.

In many written subjects, especially English, a teacher wants
to read a selection of good, interesting extracts from the work of
various pupils, or wants to refer to good points made in pieces
by a number of pupils. The activity, provided that it doesn't
follow every written assignment as regularly as clockwork, is
an excellent one. It hides, however, a trap for the unwary: how
long will it take you to find the extracts? Will you find them
in the best order to make your points? What will the pupils do
whilst they are waiting between extracts? If you are to use this
vivid didactic device, prepare it: choose and mark your passages in advance. Arrange them in the order you want, and even
rehearse a slick performance. Of course, all this applies equally
to mixed-ability as to streamed groups.

Instructions and Orders

No one can tell another person satisfactorily how to give
instructions which are accepted gracefully, understood, and
carried out. Nevertheless, it is clear that some people are better
than others, and that the technique can be learnt. The starting
point is as for talking to the class: they must *all* be silent and
still: 'Everyone please stop talking, keep quite still – stop reading, writing!' Only then give your instruction.

Consider your manner. Do not be diffident, implying by
phrase or tone that you really rather doubt if anyone is going
to obey. One teacher tried to quell a rather bouncy, noisy class
by saying in a pleasant but half-hearted voice:

'I'd like you to carry on, if you could, please. All right?'

Of course, they took no notice: and the noise went on. On the other hand, do not be unnecessarily stern or abrupt. Instruct with firmness but pleasantness. A routine instruction like 'Lead on now' can be warm and said with a smile.

Your instructions will be both more pleasant and more effective if they are, as often as possible, positive rather than negative:

'Make sure you bring a pencil tomorrow.'
rather than:
'Don't let's have so many forgotten pencils tomorrow!'

'Be absolutely punctual on Friday.'
rather than:
'Don't be so late on Friday.'

'Draw this diagram as neatly as you can.'
rather than:
'No messy work in these diagrams.'

Typical of the worst method of giving instructions is the question thrown at the whole class (while they were packing up):

'Has everyone given in their books?'

Don't turn instructions into questions. For instance, a class that is about to settle to the task of drawing a diagram may include an unknown number who have not brought the necessary pencils. If the teacher asks generally:

'Anybody need pencils?'

there will be a rash of replies from all over, including the otherwise quite unnecessary negative replies from those who *have* pencils. What's more, there is little chance of actually identifying the ones who need the pencils in the rattle of yes's and no's. Instead, the teacher should give a positive instruction, identifying those who are being addressed, and requiring hand-showing, not calling out, thus:

'Those who have *not* got pencils put your hands up, please.'

This signals that those who have got pencils need not listen further, it avoids all calling out, and it clearly shows the teacher where the pencils are wanted.

Never give a second order until the first has been obeyed. Too often a teacher shows his fear that his first instructions will be ignored by winging a second one on its way, and soon the group are deluged in a plethora of unobeyed instructions.

It is worth practising instructions on your own. Then listen to yourself as you give them in school, and observe the response. *Develop a firm warmth, or a warm firmness.*

If separate sections of a class need different points explained and practised, it is usually better to postpone the splitting until later, getting both groups to work together initially. This occurs sometimes in practical lessons, often in Music or Drama. If, for instance, the class are to sing, and half need to learn one line and half the other, teach the whole class both first. In a practical Science lesson the same applies. If half are to do one thing and half the other, explain both to the whole class first. This is educationally better, as they learn more, and it avoids the boredom of waiting.

A special example is the occasion when the teacher wishes to read out a list of rooms to which different pupils are to go, or different assignments which they are to undertake. If at all possible, don't keep the entire class waiting while you read right through the list of names. When a teacher does this, there is no way of holding the pupils' attention. The pupils whose names have been called start chatting with their friends, and this drives the pupils who are still waiting to cross reactions. The result is miserable for all. If the subject matter is not for the whole class and (unlike the song or the experiment) cannot reasonably be made for the whole class, don't try to make all listen. The alternative tactic is to give out the information individually while the class are working at something, even if it means giving the information out at an earlier moment.

Using the Blackboard

Despite years of derision from Will Hay to the de-schoolers, the blackboard (and, of course, green, white, or plastic boards for writing) remains *the* most valuable aid: it is clear, ever-ready, flexible, and unobtrusive. It requires no special black-out, and almost no special preparation. And – bulbs can't blow! You have to check only that you have a good rubber (not too hard) and chalk. Every good teacher should be at least a reasonable practitioner of the art of the board, and I shall therefore include a consideration of its technique in this section on the teacher as a performer.

As with words to the class, the basic rule is simple: think twice before use, but if you are going to use, then do so clearly and forcefully. Either the pupils need to read the message on the board or not. If not, don't distract yourself or them by writing on the board. If they do need to, ensure that what you write can be found (it isn't lost in a random corner amongst diagrams and a jumble of jottings), can be read (your writing must be large enough and clear), and can be understood (enigmatic half phrases or dark hints are useless).

It is possible to talk and write. The technique is to stand as *close* to the board as possible, with your head facing about forty-five degrees away from it. You are thus looking along the board and at least a sector of the class. Keeping your feet still, turn to the class fully at each sensible point. Of course, you would never write whole passages on the board with the pupils in the room. Its use during the lesson, then, is essentially for work in progress, words, phrases, diagrams, which you wish to illustrate spontaneously or you wish to show *changing* (e.g. adding suffixes to words). If you stand centrally, you will be forced to write standing in front of your work. If you stand too far away, you will again find that you tend to have your back fully to the class. Keep close and to one side of your work. Always start with a perfectly clear board. Well before the first pupil enters, check that the board is entirely clean and free of smudgy layers of chalk. Some cleaners will do this beautifully, but a pupil will often be a willing and meticulous 'blackboard monitor'. Check that you have a good rubber handy (old cloths are *no* use, and some proprietary rubbers need working in and softening before they will work pleasantly). Check also that there is a modest supply of the chalks you wish to use that morning (don't hoard a box full of worn scrap ends – you'll only have to scrabble through them; don't have an over-flowing gold-mine of new sticks of coloured chalks – it will tempt some of your pupils).

The key to clarity is not so much the details of your hand-writing as the disposition of your writing on the board. Establish from the first an imaginary grid on the board to give you clear columns for your writing, with real or merely visualized margins. If it is a wide board, you may need two columns. Other kinds of work would best be laid out in, perhaps, three columns. To write straight across a wide board is unwise as it is difficult to keep the line satisfactorily horizontal, and it is difficult for the pupils' eyes to carry right across the excessively long line.

Establish also conventions about the use of space on the boards. It may be that you will want to use one section always for the date, another for the instructions for the work in hand, and yet another for the homework instructions. It is often wise to reserve a section for a list of the vocabulary which you draw up during the period. There is nothing more frustrating for a pupil than to have to scan a jumbled board for a word that the teacher put up only a few moments ago and which is vital to the work in hand. I have seen some teachers flinging words in any corner of the board, overlapping, jammed up in a congested corner, and weaving through old lines and bits and pieces.

Do not 'print' (i.e. use upper case throughout) except for special purposes. The configuration of lower-case letters, with the ascenders and descenders, makes them considerably easier to read (witness the style of motorway signs). If you are likely to add words or phrases, start a column and keep to it.

Some things should be put on a board in advance: particularly diagrams, maps, lists of questions, or notes. Not only is it too difficult for most teachers to make a decent job of such work on the board without concentrating single-mindedly, but also I advise you not to get in a situation where you have to face the board for a sustained piece of drawing or writing. Particularly inept is to have to end a tricky question and answer or discussion question by a great wadge of writing on the board. Instead of the pupils being able to get straight into their work, they have to wait until the teacher has finished the first piece of writing, and even then his bobbing figure and jogging arm are distractions for most. Furthermore, just when his eye and presence are needed for settling the group into the new mood of a different style of work, he is distracted by his draughtsmanship. There are three solutions: (a) issue duplicated sheets ready prepared (in which case, keep them a secret on your desk until the dramatic moment, and then issue them briskly – cf. page 56); (b) have the material ready prepared on a ready-focused overhead projector, to be switched on at the appropriate moment (this obviously requires the transparency to have been laid on the projector and focused before the lesson); (c) prepare the material on a section of the board before the lesson, preferably a section which can be covered (by a sliding panel, revolving section, or roller board) until you want to reveal it. This revelation can be forceful and effective: it is a device as old as any, but is still very useful. Compared with (a) and (b), both of which utilize material which can be stored and used again, the use of the blackboard for extensive material is, of course, lavish with the teacher's time.

Your actual handwriting requires care: a firmly simplified hand is best, with no lavish loops. A constant firm pressure to produce a strong impression is essential. The stance while writing needs practice. Despite the advice on the previous page, it is necessary to be able to keep an eye on the class whilst writing. This requires a position facing *across* the board, so that the head can turn to the class whilst the arm is still raised. With a free-standing board or one projecting well from the wall, I find it best to stand against the side of the board. It is worth remembering that it is found by most people to be very difficult to write much below chest height. On a fixed board, therefore, regard the lowest band as unusable.

Coloured chalk is helpful if used skilfully. Eschew the pale colours as they cannot be seen easily. Yellow and red are your two best allies, with a strong green also. Blue and purple are rarely successful. Diagrams and maps apart, for they obviously have their own logic and demands, use white as your basic colour. Don't pick any old stick so that the pupils have yellow sometimes and blue at others. If you indulge in this random scatter, you will have sacrificed the effect of the deliberate use of colour. Save your alternative colours for:

> breaking up parts of words;
> underlining;
> grouping by lines or brackets;
> special lists;
> differentiating;
> etc.

Again, establish conventions suitable to your subject, your class, and you, and then keep to them. That way colour will work for you.

'Chalk and talk' has become a stupidly exaggerated pejorative phrase. So many teachers have learnt to despise any kind of teaching that could be labelled by such a tag that the profession is not retaining and improving its speaking skills. A good speaker will not necessarily be a good teacher, but the ability to communicate well in speaking is still one of the central skills of a teacher. It is curious how at a time when we are more than ever aware of the need to develop the speech of pupils, we are making them do more of their learning from reading, and less from the spoken voice and the interchange of question and answer. Similarly, the blackboard and its more modern counterpart, the overhead projector, are essential for a whole variety of lessons in a whole variety of subjects. I recommend that the pejorative implications are forgotten, and that you become as skilful as possible with 'chalk and talk'.

7 The Rhythm of Teaching

The Pattern of a Lesson

A lesson has to be organized as a sequence arranged in time, and the pattern of the learning activities must fit both the educational aims and the stretch of time available. The rhythm of these activities is an important factor under the control of the teacher. Even lessons that seem to organize themselves, such as a double Science lesson with a major practical activity, in fact require their time-sequence planning. The pupil in a school is in a time-structured environment and expects that the component elements of the day should similarly be time-structured. In my opinion, there is no escape from this demand for a use of time which is complete, intensive, and varied. The pupil is stimulated by a good use of time, and bored and irritated by a bad use. A lesson is a presentation, however much pupil participation there is, and its rhythm and pace are part of the enjoyment. When a pupil declares later in the day 'That was a good lesson!', it is frequently the pacing of the lesson which has created the feeling of satisfaction.

'Lesson planning' will eventually become an instinctive activity, even one that can continue at the back of your mind while you are doing other things. As you get more experienced and your repertoire of lesson activities grows, you will find it easier to select and to arrange almost unconsciously, only occasionally needing to write the details down. In the early days, and whenever you are on unfamiliar territory, it is worth writing down the activities and the time to be devoted to them. The key to this planning, however, is not the writing down. Many written lesson plans look good at first glance, but are worse than useless in their inaccuracy of conception. The key is the ability to think through a lesson in advance, as it were to preview rapidly the entire stretch of time. This is an imaginative feat that takes in the learning activities, the nature of the room and its facilities, the pupil group and its key individuals, and the occasion of the day. In some ways, teachers of Science are helped by their burdensome equipment demands, which force them to specify their precise needs to the lab technicians in advance, and then to visualize the whole lesson. Such an approach is required, however, by all teachers. (On page 88 I give an example of a skeleton lesson plan.)

You will start by considering the clock length of your lessons: thirty, thirty-five, forty, fifty, or sixty-minute periods are all to be found in different schools, and whereas some schools use double (or triple) periods only for 'practical' subjects, others have an extensive use of doubles for very many if not most subjects. Obviously, a double forty-minute lesson gives a period of one hour and twenty minutes. This is a long stretch of time and needs careful apportioning. There is certainly evidence that teachers use shorter sessions more intensively than longer ones, and I sometimes think that moves towards longer periods, which are embarked on for the best of motives, are reduced in effectiveness by a sharp drop in the intensity of the use of time, and a consequent increase in pupil boredom.

The effective length of time will obviously depend on the pattern of pupil movement. If, as with younger classes in some Secondary schools, the teacher moves to the class, and if, for instance, the period is the second single of two, the teacher can work to virtually the whole of the clock time. If, as is more common, the pupils move to the teacher's room, there has to be a reasonable deduction for movement. You should work out the effective length of the lesson, and then consider how it can be broken down. It is important to think always of what the pupils will be *doing* at a given moment, and to visualize how one activity joins to the next.

Every lesson needs a shape, and its shape is made up of the units of time into which it is divided. The relationship between these units creates the rhythm. I don't want to over-elaborate this way of looking at teaching, but I would stress the immense value of rhythmic variety. You can represent typical lesson rhythm diagramatically in this way:

(*a* i) Conventional use of double periods:

exposition	activity	conclusion

Sometimes there are two preludes:

(b i)

work handed back	exposition or stimulus	activity	conclusion

My comments would be that both these are acceptable patterns, but both have their faults, and neither should be over-used. Certainly, (ai) is far too often the basic rhythm of Science lesson after lesson, and (bi) is too often the standard pattern of innumerable English lessons. Both have their objections. For a double period, the central activity in (a i) is very often too long in relation to the range of activities involved, and in proportion to the sandwich of exposition and conclusion. (b i) suffers from two starting units which are too similar: it is frequently nearly impossible to get the pupils into the activity after such a repeated false start. As a variant on (a i) I would suggest:

(a ii)

initial activity	explanation and exposition	main activity	final summary

In this case there is a brief introductory activity ready laid out with instructions to start the lesson and *precede* the main exposition, which is now reinforced by some activity in advance. (This may, of course, be practical, or it may involve writing as a precursor to the lesson.) Yet a further alternative to (a i) would be this:

(a iii)

main activity	explanation	writing

In which case the main activity has to be entered in upon cold, presuming that directions and apparatus are clear enough for this to be possible. In pattern (a iii) the writing occupies a final stretch of time of maybe twenty minutes, and is designed for pondering the activity and letting its conclusions sink in. (I am convinced that far too often pupils rush straight into the playground from an activity, without an opportunity for it to 'register'.) This final section will be used for clearing up and putting away, as well as providing an opportunity for the teacher to go over points quietly with one or two pupils.

As an occasional alternative to (*b* i) I should offer:

(*b* ii)

Exposition or stimulus	activity	work handed back

This avoids the problem of the double start, although it risks too long an activity section for it to be suitable for all occasions. It would work if the balance between the three units was right. A further variation is this:

Exposition or stimulus	initial activity	work handed back	main activity

This allows the lesson to be 'played out' with the main activity, which is especially suitable if it is to lead straight into home-work (but see my point about dating on page 38). Presuming that you *want* a group handing–back of work on this occasion (there may well be times when you would prefer to hand it back individually with a quiet private word), I have suggested as a variation that this is inserted *after* the main activity has been started. Such a break can, of course, be jerkily irritating. How-ever, it can sometimes be effective and justified. I have, for instance, often noticed how many times a run of work is actu-ally broken by the teacher's interpolated comments. If you do this, capitalize on the break, make something of it, and draw some relevant points from the work being handed back.

Whatever your views on the six patterns I have just sketched, I hope that you will agree that there are a number of varia-tions of pace and rhythm, and that lessons should not settle monotonously into only one pattern. The variations should be used both for functional relevance to the nature of the learning activity, and also for the sheer value of variety.

Here is an example of pre-lesson plan jottings. This was to be a Maths lesson on arrow diagrams in the SMP syllabus, with a number of sections. The double lesson was after break, which ended nominally at 11.15. The times on the right are finish-ing times to help the teacher see roughly when each section should be completed. You will notice that there were five minutes in hand, as the final bell went at 12.35. (By the way, never keep a class in except as a punishment: they resent being late out.)

On the board in advance:
    starter instructions;
    key words (ringed in teacher's book);
    my arrow diagram;
    family tree.

Timing (2 × 40 = 80)	time:	finish by:
Starter on paper	5	11.20
Intro: 'What are we doing?'	5	11.25
New work on board	5	11.30
Silent study of p. 103 a, b, c,	15	11.45
Oral questions and answers and		
explanation on those	15	12.00
Written exercise p. 105	20	12.20
Final summary and questions	10	12.30
	75	

∴ five minutes spare

n.b. collect books

Of course, the wise teacher does not keep rigidly to his pre-planned shape. He will judge the mood of the class and the response to the learning activity. He may well continue a successful activity for considerably longer than he had planned; he certainly may abandon intended sections; he may have 'reserve' activities available; he may even insert a spontaneous activity. Such flexibility is obviously necessary as the success or even the timing of a part of a lesson cannot be gauged fully in advance. Yet this flexibility should not be too great. If, for instance, an explanation to the class is proving more difficult than anticipated, and therefore taking longer, it could well be wiser, nevertheless, to keep to the plan for the lesson, sum up the explanation achieved so far, and leave it for this occasion, returning to the topic in the next lesson. This is not always possible – for a fair understanding of the topic may be essential for the remainder of that session's learning activity. However, it can be disastrous to abandon the plan and plug away at the explanation, thus destroying the texture of time. A contrasting example would be a lesson that was to have had in it a limited period of writing. The teacher finds that when it comes to the time at which he had planned to break off the writing and read some fresh material to the class, play a tape, or present a summary, all the pupils are miraculously engrossed in their writing, and it seems a tragedy to break the concentration. On such an occasion he may be wise to capitalize on the flow of energy, scrap the next planned activity, and let the writing continue. However, I should caution against too great a flexibility even here. The extra time you can offer on this occasion is probably insufficient for the work to be completed; if you abandon your plan and allow the writing to continue, you might well find it petering out before the end of the lesson, with an awkward gap left. Finally, the teacher, as much as the music-hall performer or the television star, does well to remember that the customer is often better satisfied if he is left wanting more. Better a class saying 'Why can't we go on writing?' than one desperately longing for the writing to end.

The pupil also needs to know where the lesson is going, how much of the time he will have in which to choose his own activity, how long he will spend on an exercise in Mathematics, or what proportion of the period will be devoted to full-class question and answer in a language lesson. For too many pupils, most lessons are a more or less exciting mystery tour, in which they never know how long they are going to be at one activity before they are set down or whipped off for another. The teacher needs to include 'signposts' in a lesson.

Activity

It is the oldest and one of the most sensible of teachers' sayings that pupils must have something to *do*. This is so for two complementary reasons: in the first place, we all learn most firmly by doing (especially if the actions are preceded and reinforced by verbal explanation and by the pupil's own verbalization). It is worth realizing that this is so even of the purely routine copying: it is a form of action which reinforces learning more definitely than listening or reading. In the second place, pupils enjoy doing things, and on the whole don't much enjoy listening whilst other pupils say things. (They prefer listening to Sir.)[1]

The experienced teacher makes sure that every lesson offers ample opportunity for activity, and that there is ample activity for each pupil, whatever his ability. These activities should be

[1] The preliminary results of the research of the Schools Council's 'Extending Reading Project' suggest that as much as 38 per cent of the time in English and some other humanity lessons is spent *listening*.

cunningly placed in the lesson. For instance, I have already suggested that there should often be an initial activity as the first section, however short, of a lesson. The purpose of this initial activity may be to get the pupils thinking, to raise questions in their minds. Thus its full understanding may depend on a later synthesis and explanation.

If there is to be a long stretch of activities, it is important that the directions (on board, overhead projector, or worksheet) should be *clear enough for the majority of the class to move on without having to ask questions.* There is nothing more ruinous of the rhythm of a lesson than the constipated jerkiness of pupils who cannot move ahead without further help.

In mixed-ability classes, especially, it is obviously important that each sequence of activities should start with ones that are simple enough for all, and, conversely, that there are others difficult enough to stretch the most able, and sufficient of them. Never underestimate the pleasure, satisfaction, and educational value which pupils get from satisfactorily completing an action, *however simple.* This is especially true of techniques like certain measurements in Mathematics, aspects of map reading, or experiments in Science.

It is worth spending time thinking up activities to help *towards* the teaching of a fact or a skill. It is a frequent mistake to want the pupils to learn the real point too early: a set of 'limbering up' activities is most valuable. For instance, how would you help the pupils to learn about contours or paragraphs? Or how would you prepare them for measuring temperatures? In both cases a mere identifying exercise is a valuable starter. In the first case, to 'trace over in a brown pencil the contour lines on this map' (and it will have been specially drawn for simplicity). In the second example, have the pupils mark with a red pencil all the paragraph indentations in a photo-stencilled page or two from a printed book. In the third, have them look at duplicated reproductions of a thermometer scale, and write in the scale points. The art of teaching includes the art of devising such activities.

Variety is as important in the activities devised as it is in the over-all rhythm of the lesson. For instance, a current fault is to offer young Secondary pupils an interminable diet of worksheets, so that the activities are the same not merely throughout the lesson, but also from lesson to lesson. This soon palls – especially if, as too often happens, your colleagues are similarly addicted to worksheets in other subject areas. 'Individual learning', far from being a panacea, can be a yawning bore – it relies on good reading, good motivation, and good behaviour. It gives insufficient teacher feedback to the majority of pupils, and leaves dozens with their hands up for long sections of the day.

Stillness and Movement

For most lessons there are sections which are more or less still and quiet and sections which are more or less active and noisy. One of the arts of patterning is to vary these elements. In the early years of adolescence – indeed, I should say right through to the end of compulsory schooling – pupils can rarely take too much of one or the other. The mixture needs to be varied. In a Humanities lesson, discussion, question-and-answer, cutting and sticking activities are clearly times of noise and activity, whereas reading, writing, or various kinds of worksheets are basically still and quiet. In Science, there is an obvious similar distinction between group experiments, which thrive on bustle and conversation, and noting down, measuring, and writing, which require peace. In languages, there is the contrast between oral work and writing.

My first advice is to exaggerate rather than to blur these distinctions. The variety of the rhythm will be less attractive if the activities are indistinguishable, and if there is always dead hush and stillness (a rare fault this, however!) or a general wash of noise and movement throughout everything (a much more common difficulty). Part of the value of the still sections is precisely their contrast with the more active ones. Play the variations with a musician's skill. Sometimes have your stillness for a long central section; at other times start with a calm still section; and at other times make your coda a final fifteen minutes of stillness. To open with a still section is often the easiest for a young teacher, who finds the task of getting quiet out of noise more difficult. It is surprising, therefore, that it is not more often used. I recommend that there should be 'still' work to hand as pupils come in, with the work on the desk, directions given personally to them as they enter, and the instructions confirmed by a clear direction already on the board. Start a double period with twenty minutes of that – rather than the movement of handing back some writing with your verbal comments. Above all, pattern the variations of stillness and movement, of quiet and of voices, as a deliberate part of the rhythm of the lesson, for the rhythm of the lesson can support the teaching aim and help the learner.

Summing Up

Almost every learning session benefits from a final 'summing up'. Apart from anything else, pupils who have been obliged to spend, say, an hour and twenty minutes in a room are happier if they are reminded before leaving of what they have achieved. They need, as it were, the final signpost or arrival board. At a carefully judged point near the end, the attention of the whole group should usually be gained. This may be the very last task before the clock indicates that it is time to go; it may be prior to 'clearing up'; it may, less often, be the penultimate activity, and the lesson session may end with a final fifteen minutes of quiet activity. The teacher, having gained the undivided attention of the pupils, should briskly, and with praise if this is at all justifiable, run over what has been learnt or otherwise achieved:

> 'Today almost everyone has completed their long story, and we seem to have an impressive collection already.'
> 'Now we have really got that point about contour lines quite clear.'
> 'You've all done valuable work from the cards today. This means we've all learnt something about how we measure heat.'

It is obviously important not to use the summing up to embark on a fresh lesson. However, it is usually possible to pick up the salient features of the session, highlight the contributions of a few members of the group, and as it were give the group back their achievement so that they can feel something has been achieved. This rounding-off must not be allowed to become a mere empty routine, but usually it is a wise final shot – especially in a lesson which, perhaps with a mixed-ability group, has been largely occupied with individual assignments. On many occasions the pupils should participate in this, either in brief question-and-answer, or in a prepared statement. There will, however, also be occasions when it is better to leave a loose end or two to tie up the following day with a bright introduction.

Fillers

An experienced teacher has a store of 'fillers' which can be slipped into the last five or ten minutes of a lesson. A lesson must end if not with a bang at least with a definite note. Too many fritter away with a whimper. If it seems likely that there is to be time left, instead of stretching the material out desperately, compress it. Keeping an eye on the clock, draw the threads together earlier than planned; go through your clearing up and closing routine (see page 50) briskly and energetically, and then, with the lesson completely finished and five minutes to go, launch briefly into your 'filler'. This can be based on old material from your subject presented in the form of question-and-answer, or a game, one side of the class against the other. It can be based on puzzles derived from your subject, or from words which are part of your subject. This is an excellent moment for a brief reading of a poem, incident, or description that you know well and which in some way links with the class's interests. It is a good moment for each to jot down a couple of words in answer to some question. This is even a time when some aspect of school routine, future planning, or class business can be introduced. Indeed it may be time for a disconnected activity based on words, number, or general knowledge for an intelligent, brisk ending. Two warnings: don't use 'fillers' too often – they lose their function; and keep them very brief: like a pre-faded track on a television programme, their climax should precisely synchronize with the clock.

The Rhythm of a Sequence of Lessons

I have been speaking of the rhythm of a lesson. It is important to stress that I am not recommending that there is one 'ideal' rhythm for a group. Despite my emphasis on routines and procedures for a class, it is vital that there is rhythmic variety between lessons. If you meet a class, for instance, for two doubles in a week, you should sense the need to vary the pattern, perhaps having five basic patterns, four of which you use in every fortnight. A class, such as Mathematics, which meets for five or more periods each week, migh well benefit from one session each week having a fixed and routine pattern – it might be a test, a silent reading period, or a serious story. Such a 'fixed feast' gives the teacher a respite from planning and the pupils a known resting point. But the other four sessions need varying so that the tempo is neither known nor repetitive.

One of the major skills of a teacher is a highly developed inner clock, which he uses to pace the activities, not in a merely mechanical way, but in a subtle, almost aesthetic pattern. Rhythmic variety and suitability contribute to effective teaching.

Conserving Energy

Learn to pace your day and your weeks. I remember hearing John Gielgud say in a radio interview that the key to playing King Lear was to pace the part, so that one had sufficient physical and emotional energy in reserve for the later climaxes. The same is true of teaching. You will have around thirty periods to teach each week. You cannot afford to prepare too many of those in great detail: you will not have time. You cannot allow too many of them to involve great vocal strain: you won't have any voice left. You cannot work too hard in too many: you will be exhausted before the end of each day. For much of this book I have been inevitably concerned with the individual learning session, a period or double period. Similarly, the young teacher's concerns tend to focus on the problems of managing a single session. To a degree this is wise, for the first target is clearly to become proficient at leading a successful lesson. However, in time it becomes clear that the real problem is not the individual session, but the run of lessons over a month or half a term. This is what creates the pupils' learning experiences. More immediately, though, the teacher needs to consider the longer sequence from his own point of view. He must learn to conserve his energy if he is to give of his best consistently. Too often, young teachers find it difficult to cope because of frayed nerves and flagging energy. Obviously one expects to be tired at the end of a week's work, but if the tiredness is welling up mid-week and mid-day and seriously hampering effective handling of the classroom, then something is wrong with the individual's pacing of the week. You have to work hard to keep fresh. You cannot afford to get over-tired.

The Sequence of the Year

Pupils need to know that they are going somewhere. It is therefore wise to take them into your confidence with the plan of the year, how it links with what has gone before, and what it leads on to. If possible, create opportunities for choice within this framework so that they have a hand in their own destiny. Create as much variety of texture as you can over the year, so that week after week is not an interminable routine. Mark out clearly any stages reached, and make it clear that progress is being made.

Inevitably, I have spoken about what the teacher does, and I have described situations from the teacher's point of view. Of course, it is the pupil's learning that matters, and in the end the test is not what you've taught, but what the pupil has actually learned. A teacher will develop ways of picking up the clues of expressions, remarks, actions, and questions to gauge how well the pupils have learnt. The teacher will further supplement this by deliberate assessment procedures, whether they are a simple question in a Science lesson, a rapid check of words learnt in a Modern Language lesson, a quiz, or a more definite test. Sciences, Languages, and Mathematics need frequent modest assessment procedures, not for grading the pupils, but to provide a feedback to the teacher. From this feedback the teacher will both vary the learning experiences and give a feedback to the pupils so that they have a sense of progress – a necessary feeling.

8 Preparing Yourself

You will hear often the need to 'prepare your lessons', and I have extended this to preparing a range of aspects of the room and the routine. Finally, though, there are ways in which a teacher needs to prepare himself more personally. In this section I shall suggest how your skill in the classroom needs to be supported by personal preparation.

Using the School

To work from a position of strength it is necessary for you to feel completely sure of the school context into which your personal work fits. Some schools are fairly good at making their routines and procedures clear through explicit documentation and briefing sessions, but it must be admitted that this is one of the weakest aspects of educational organization.

If a school does produce a 'Staff Handbook' or any other organizational documentation, obviously you should study it carefully. Some procedures may be arbitrary; more have probably grown out of particular points of the locality, building, organizational structure, timetabling scheme, etc. It is wise to presume that there is a reason for everything, and to find out that reason if possible. Later, you may wish to join in discussions to modify or completely change those procedures. However, whilst they stand, operate them punctiliously. If all the teachers in the school work to the same procedures, each is supporting the other.

Soon after your appointment, arrange a visit to the school to find out as much as you can. The key figure to get to know closely is your Head of Department. (If you are to be given pastoral responsibility, the Head of Year or Head of House for whom you will be working is also most important.) From your Head of Department you will want a scheme of work, copies of the main books with which you will be working, and details of the classes and the timetable.

You will want to find out the communication and responsibility pattern of the school. What is the role of each of the senior staff? Therefore, to whom do you refer what? What is the procedure for supporting you if you have difficulties in the classroom? What supervisory duties will you be asked to undertake, and who will guide you in them?

Your departmental team should give you specialist support in your subject teaching. You can expect to discuss all your problems with the Head of Department, from pupils to equipment, from rooms to routines. Make sure that you put your worries to him or her as early as possible. If you are unlucky enough to work under an unusual Head of Department who does not offer this kind of help, turn to one of the Deputy Heads instead.

Watch other colleagues at work, especially those in different disciplines. An English teacher, for instance, has a great deal to learn from the techniques of exposition of a Maths teacher; a Humanities teacher can often learn from the handling of practical and group work in a Science lesson; a Science teacher may learn much from the structured discussion techniques of an English teacher.

Being in Training

A great deal depends on the inner calm of the teacher. It is almost as if a teacher needs to be in physical and psychological training for the classroom. If you are tired, worried, torn apart with inner stress, or hectic from rushing, it is extremely difficult to keep your cool in the classroom. A group of adolescents is both demanding and challenging to be with, whatever classroom mode you are using. You will not be able to cope with them if you cannot cope with yourself!

It may seem both irrelevant and impertinent to offer advice about evenings and weekends in a book about the teacher's management of the classroom. However, it is a very real fact that the dynamic of a teacher's working year is very different from that of, say, an office worker. It is no good the teacher merely moaning about the awful stresses of teaching and how no other job is as wearing. Success in the classroom depends, amongst other things, upon realizing fairly precisely in what ways a teacher's lot is a *different* one, and taking those differences into account.

There are really two crucial differences: one is the pattern of responsibility and the other is the pattern of time. Young teachers who have listened carefully to lectures and seminars about 'the deprived child' and have considered conscientiously the learning needs of children, nevertheless find the shock of actual responsibility for them very great indeed. It is, in fact, an open-ended responsibility, for the needs of children are so great that there is never a clear stopping point where you can mentally tick a task off as 'completed'. And the more sensitive and conscientious you are, the more aware you will be of the inevitable sense of failure and the more appalled by the never-ending vista of further needs. This nagging responsibility is quite unlike many a professional or commercial responsibility, which is for some part of a process: if the individual carries out his task skilfully, others take the final responsibility. In those jobs, the individual can hand his task on, and dispatch it from his mind also. Not so the teacher. This constant sense of unfulfilled responsibility drives some teachers to cynicism, others to frantically continuous political action, others to almost neurotic preparation of teaching materials, and others to despair. You must cope with it by working hard when you are working, but learn to switch off and take up your private pursuits at other times. Overcome by the emotional impact of the open-ended responsibilities, too many teachers sit and brood, chewing over the pupils' needs, and wasting time and nervous energy regretting that they cannot do more for them. You must be able to switch off.

The pattern of time needs reflecting upon also. I am not prepared to say that over the year as a whole the conscientious teacher puts in more hours than his or her opposite number in some other comparable occupation. What is true, however, is that that time is put in more unevenly, and this needs planning for. University and College of Education life, with its even longer holidays, latish mornings, and comparatively relaxed days, is very poor training for the school teaching week. The number of days in which you do not have to attend school is high, but the amount of work that you need to get through in a teaching week is also very high – and it won't wait for attention later! The intensity of the day is very great. Consider the gradual way a Monday morning gets going in some offices: a number of people come in rather later; there is less work waiting in the in-trays; coffee break can be a trifle longer and the weekend discussed; even the lunch hour can be extended. I find many teachers, on the other hand, suffer from Sunday-evening pangs, as a creeping worry about the next morning's work starts filling up the back of the mind. Preparations for the week's work loom ahead, and are frequently started too late, or pushed aside. Either way, and even if the work has actually been done, it is difficult not to be vaguely depressed about the inadequacy and at the same time vaguely resentful about the loss of weekend time.

The only hope, I am sure, is to organize your year, your week, and your day around these factors of responsibility and the use of time. Plan family reunions, visits, theatre trips and the like for holiday periods; keep school week nights fairly free of social engagements, especially those parties and meals attended by people who do not have to be at work early the following morning. Don't allow the first week of a holiday to drift by with neither work nor pleasure fitted in. Many teachers feel they need a week to 'run down'. I personally think they waste precious parts of the year like this. I should recommend going into school *at the usual time* on the day immediately after term for a vigorous day's work in the peace of an empty school, tying up loose ends, tidying your drawers and cupboards, taking down old displays, and reorganizing equipment and books. If you can, finish any outstanding marking *that day* or the next – it is deeply depressing to have piles of unread pupils' work on your sitting-room table and the need to mark them on your mind for the rest of the holiday. If possible, arrange your 'holiday' part of the holiday to follow this brief spell of intensive terminal effort. That way, you will not fritter away precious days, and the complete break and change will be refreshing. Finally, if any substantial work is required before the next term, do it as early as possible after your holiday, so that the final weekend before term can again be a complete break.

Similarly deliberate tactics are necessary during a term-time week. Relegate as many personal evening activities as you can to Fridays or Saturdays. If you are to be ready to start work with the necessary full vigour at nine o'clock in the morning (unlike most jobs when the 'starting time' is really only an arrival time), you must be fresh, and for most people this means few or no late nights. When school has ended, try to spend a short while at least with one or two of your pupils, and try to fit in one after-school pupil activity a week. But when you arrive home, try not to slip into 'the teacher evening': 'I'm too tired to do anything, even relax'. You will almost certainly have some reading of pupils' work or lesson preparation. Do it early in the evening, and then forget school.

A successful teaching term requires, for most people, a fairly ruthless organization of their private lives.

Conclusion

The development of subject specialism has contributed a great deal to the Secondary school in the last two decades. However, the curriculum development that has come with it has tended to lead teachers to under-value general teaching skills, and to over-rely on expertise in a particular subject area and on suitability of 'material'. In this book I have emphasized that there are general teaching skills which are applicable to most subject areas, to most lesson techniques, and in most schools. These are, furthermore, *school* teaching skills, and essential to the particular learning conditions of Secondary schools, however they may change. The aspects of 'craft' that I have outlined emphatically refer to mixed-ability as well as more homogeneous groups and to pupil-centred teaching approaches as well as the more specifically didactic.

There is, of course, no simple answer, no single remedy, and certainly no complete success. With some situations a range of remedies has to be simultaneously applied, and the most that can be hoped for is a partial success. When a teacher is having difficulty, the problems often seem so great that he would very much like the whole burden to disappear quietly. It doesn't, though. What's more, the longer one carries it as a vast amorphous problem, the heavier it becomes as a burden. The only hope is to take it to pieces and see where improvements can be made. Work at the details section by section.

You will sometimes feel you have succeeded, but disappointments will be frequent. I know only too well that some people could conscientiously apply all the detail I've listed and yet not get across at all. The craft won't work without a spirit compounded of the salesman, the music-hall performer, the parent, the clown, the intellectual, the lover, and the organizer, but the spirit won't win through on its own either. Method matters. The more 'organized' you are, the more sympathetic you can be. The better your classroom management, the more help you can be to your pupils.

Appendix: Some Helpful Books

Barnes, D., Britton, J. Rosen, H., *Language, the Learner and the School*, Penguin, 1971.

Blackburn, Keith, *The Tutor*, Heinemann Organization in Schools Series, 1975.

Clegg, Alec, and Megson, Barbara, *Children in Distress*, Penguin, 1968.

Herber, Harold L., *Reading in Content Areas*, Prentice–Hall, 1970.

Holt, John, *How Children Fail*, Penguin, 1960.

Leggat, Robert, *Lights Please! Using Projector in the Classroom*, National Committee for Audio-visual Aids in Education, 1974. A practical handbook which covers all uses of projectors, including straightforward projecting of films and creation uses.

Leggat, R., *'Showing Off' or Display Techniques for the teacher*, National Committee for Audio-visual Aids in Education, 1970.

Marland, Michael, *Pastoral Care*, Heinemann Organization in Schools Series, 1974.

McFarland, H. S. N., *Intelligent Teaching, Professional Skills for Student Teachers*, Routledge & Kegan Paul, 1973. Although written only for those on teaching practice, this book is possibly of even greater interest to those in their early years, as Professor McFarland's synthesis for theory and practice is stimulating and helpful to those with some experience.

National Union of Teachers, *Treasure Chest*, Schoolmaster Publishing Co.

Richardson, Elizabeth, *The Environment of Learning*, Heinemann Organization in Schools Series, 1973.

Shipman, Martin, *Childhood – a sociological perspective*, NFER, 1972.

Turner, Barry (ed.), *Discipline in Schools*, Ward Lock Educational, 1973.

Wall, W. D., *Adolescents in School and Society*, NFER, 1968.

Weston, John, *The Tape-recorder in the Classroom*, National Committee for Audio-visual Aids in Education, 1974.

Index